Litera
Objec

1

David McLaughlin

PEARSON
Longman

Pearson Education
Edinburgh Gate
Harlow
Essex
CM20 2JE

England and Associated Companies throughout the World

ISBN 0 582 52990 5

First published 2002
Fourth impression 2003

Printed in Great Britain by Scotprint, Haddington

The publisher's policy is to use paper manufactured from sustainable forests.

Cover: Kelly Harriger/Corbis.

Sources and acknowledgements

Texts

We are grateful to the following for permission to reproduce copyright material:

A P Watt Limited on behalf of The National Trust for Places of Historical Interest or Natural Beauty for the poem 'If' by Rudyard Kipling; Essential Books Limited for an extract from the 'Fork Handles' sketch by Ronnie Barker published in All I Ever Wrote © Ronnie Barker; Faber and Faber Limited for the poem 'Macavity: The Mystery Cat' by T S Eliot published in Old Possum's Book of Practical Cats; FremantleMedia Limited for the use of a game-show format; Guardian Newspapers Limited for an extract from the on-line debate 'Should Humans be Cloned?' by Tim Radford and Dr Robin Lovell-Badge published at www.guardian.co.uk 4th August 2001 © The Guardian 2001; Laurence Pollinger Limited for the poem 'To a Cat' by Jorge Luis Borges; Penguin Books Limited for an extract from Carrie's War by Nina Bawden © Nina Bawden 1973; and Saddle Skedaddle for an extract adapted from their website www.skedaddle.demon.co.uk on UK Skedaddle weekends.

In some instances we have been unable to trace the owners of copyright material and we would appreciate any information that would enable us to do so.

Photographs

Photo from www.JohnBirdsall.co.uk: p.6 (top); Gareth Boden Photography: p.107; Kim Taylor/Bruce Coleman Collection: p.136; Donald Cooper/Photostage: pp.132, 134; Corbis: pp.41, 42 (left), 44, 46, 48; Bettmann/Corbis: p.97; Kelly Harriger/Corbis: pp.49, 50, 52, 54, 56; Digital Progression: pp.75, 76, 78, 80, 82; Getty Images/Ken Chernus: p.88; Getty Images/Paul Harris: p.77; Getty Images/Bill Ling: p.6 (bottom left).

Sally Greenhill: pp.6 (bottom right), 8, 10, 12 (left), 20; Amblin Entertainment/Universal/Ronald Grant: pp.101, 102, 104, 106, 108; Kobal Collection/Amblin/Universal: p.103; Saddle Skeddadle for the logos p.69 (top left); Saddle Skeddadle/Caroline Griffiths: p.69 (right), Saddle Skeddadle/Andrew Straw: pp.67, 68, 69 (left), 70, 71, 72 (left), 74.

Permission to reproduce holiday logos p.72: 'This picture was provided by Butlins Skyline Ltd', 'Pontin's', 'MyTravel Group', 'Credited to Thomas Cook'.

Permission to reproduce front covers p.12: BECKHAM, photography by Dean Freeman, design by Grace, ©Footwork Productions Limited 2001.

GERI HALLIWELL, reproduced with the kind permission of Transworld Publishers. All rights reserved.

Picture Research by Sandie Huskinson-Rolfe of PHOTOSEEKERS.

Illustrations by: Philip Hurst p.15; John Holder p.23; John Ireland p.31; Andy Hamilton pp.35, 93, 99; Oxford Designers and Illustrators p.51; Ron Tiner pp.57, 119; David Kearney p.83; Sam Hadley p.109; Diane Fawcett p.127; David Roberts p.135.

Contents

Get it right

Unit 1: Plan, draft and present

Planning and drafting are essential stages in the writing process. You also want to **present** your reader with a carefully written piece of writing, sometimes including appropriate diagrams, pictures and illustrations.

 P Plan

Research

You are going to plan, draft and present a piece of writing about your life when you were a young child. You are going to research the following:

▶ where and when you were born

▶ how much you weighed, your length, etc.

▶ what parents and other family members said at the time

▶ what was happening in the world the year you were born – for example in sport, music and politics

▶ what you were like as a baby

▶ your favourite toys.

1 How are you going to find out about your early life?

2 What books and other sources of information are you going to use to find out about the year in which you were born?

Thinking about your reading

How do you make sense of what you are reading? When you are looking for information, what methods do you use to select important details and reject unimportant ones? Look at this encyclopaedia entry about the Internet.

The <u>Internet, a series of interconnected computer networks,</u> is changing the way people communicate. The <u>Internet enables a person at one computer to communicate with people all over the world</u>. It was originally <u>created by the United States Department of Defense</u>. In the last few years the Internet has grown explosively – from approximately 200 network sites in 1981 to 50,000 in 1995.

Anyone who has access to a computer with a modem can gain access to the Internet. On the Internet they can read information, join discussions, or communicate by e-mail. Businesses also use the Internet to sell their products and services.

A way of identifying the key information is to **skim-read** the article to get to the important facts. Then we can highlight the key words to reveal the information we want. The underlined words in the encyclopaedia entry help to answer the question 'What is the Internet?'

1 Copy out the second paragraph of the article and underline the words that help answer the question 'What can you do on the Internet?'

2 Find out information about the year in which you were born. By skim-reading the information, identify the key points. Make the key points you have found stand out by underlining or recording them separately.

Making notes

When you have found all the answers to your questions about your life when you were a young child, you are going to need to put together some notes. Here are two methods you could use.

Example

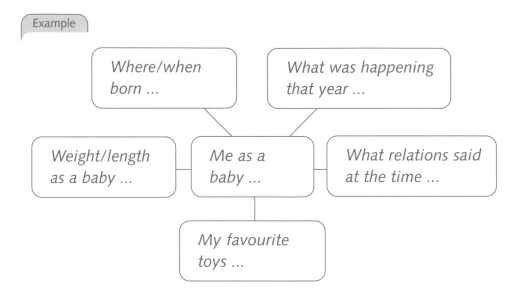

Where/when born ...

What was happening that year ...

Weight/length as a baby ...

Me as a baby ...

What relations said at the time ...

My favourite toys ...

Example

Me	Notes
When and where I was born	
My weight and length at birth	
What relations said at the time	
What was happening in the year I was born	
What I was like as a baby	
Favourite toys	

1 Choose one of the note-making methods above and use it to record the information you have gathered.

Checking your sources

When researching a topic it is important to keep a note of where you found the information. It is important that you use sources that you can rely on to give you accurate information.

In 1990 Madonna got to No.1 with her song 'Vogue'. Look at the following information sources.

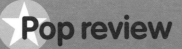

Pop review

The new single from Madonna is 'Vogue', a cheesy attempt to jump on the dance bandwagon. The singing is poor and the tune non-existent. It's got as much chance of going to No.1 in the charts as I have of becoming Prime Minister!

interview

"I remember lots of brilliant No.1s this year, but the one I liked the best was Madonna's 'Vogue'."

1990
The year in pop music

This has been an excellent year for dance music, with lots of new faces like Seal jumping into the charts, as well as established acts like Madonna taking the top spot in the single chart with her dance-inspired anthem 'Vogue'.

Letter to pop magazine

I'm a big Madonna fan, but she won't get to No.1 with the awful dance song 'Vogue'.

1 Which of these information sources could you rely on to give you accurate information about whether 'Vogue' reached No.1? Give reasons for your answer.

2 For your own research, make a note of the places where you would expect to find reliable information.

3 How can you be sure that the information you have gathered so far is accurate?

D Draft

Organising your material

You are now ready to write an outline of your autobiography. This is where your notes start to take shape and you begin to see the overall structure of the final piece of writing emerge.

1 Organise the information you have gathered into four main points. These four points will form the basis of your piece of writing.

Example

Details of my birth
- *born 4th January 1990 in Manchester*
- *weighed 8 lb*
- *My mum said I looked like an angel*

What I was like as a baby
- *cried a lot*
- *always putting things in the bin*
- *trying to crawl*

Likes/dislikes
- *Thomas the Tank Engine* ✓
- *Barbie* ✗

What was happening in the world that year
- *Madonna at No. 1*
- *Man Utd won the Cup*

Writing a first draft

The first draft is where you attempt to write the whole piece for the first time. After you have completed it you will want to make changes to it to make the writing clearer. You might also want to add more details and use more descriptive language, whilst also checking your spelling and punctuation.

Pr Present

Presenting the final draft

Your final presentation could involve a variety of different elements and may be produced in a number of ways. It could be handwritten or produced using a computer. It could be a mixture of words, diagrams, pictures and illustrations.

A typical webpage might be presented like this:

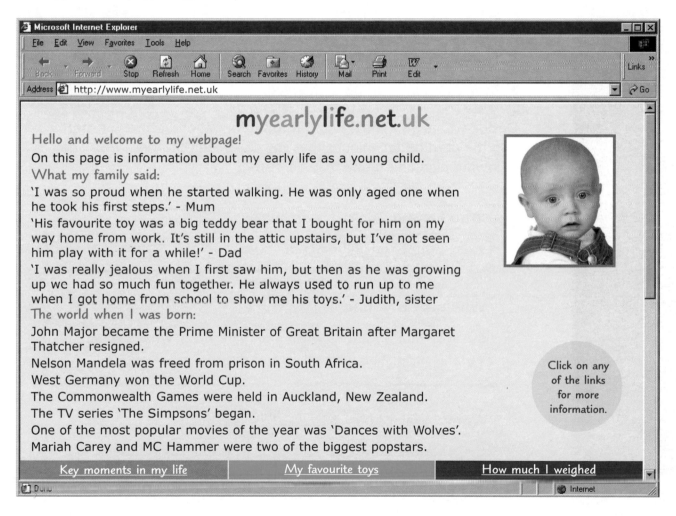

1 Design your own Internet webpage showing some of the information that you have gathered about your life as a young child.

Writing an autobiography

You are now going to write your own autobiography. Use the notes you have from your research. You will also need to do some new research about your life **now.** A main focus of the autobiography will be the difference between what you thought when you were a small child and what you think now. Also mention the changes in your life and in the world since you were a small child.

You might want to find out about:

▶ friends and favourite teachers at primary school

▶ memorable holidays or days out

▶ how you felt about leaving primary school

▶ how you think you have changed.

Decide where you could find out this information before you start. Use the drafting techniques that you used earlier to help you. The following planning frame may be of use:

Introduction

Explain what you will describe in your autobiography.

When I was young

Give information about when you were born, what people thought about you, your likes and dislikes.

When I was older

Give information about your time at primary school and the change to secondary school. Tell the reader about any memorable events.

How I have changed

Explain the main differences between how you were as a young child and how you are now. Describe how you feel about them.

When you have completed your draft, you need to decide how to present your autobiography. Are you going to handwrite it or use a word processor? You also need to decide whether to use pictures, illustrations and diagrams.

You could use the writing frame below to help you to organise your writing:

> ▶ I was born on …
> ▶ In the year I was born important events in the world were …

> ▶ When I was born people in my family said …
> ▶ They also said …

> ▶ I am told that as a baby I …
> ▶ Now I realise, however, that I was …

> ▶ My favourite toys were …
> ▶ Now I think that these toys are …
> ▶ The things that I like now include …

> ▶ When I was a young child I thought that …
> ▶ I also believed that …
> ▶ I realise now that …

> ▶ Some important events when I was growing up included …

> ▶ My friends at primary school were …
> ▶ My feelings about them then were …

> ▶ When I left primary school to come to secondary school, I felt …
> ▶ I now feel …

Review of skills

Spelling log ▶▶▶

Improving your spelling is not just a matter of learning words for a weekly test, it is also an important part of becoming a better writer.

▶ Whenever you come across an unfamiliar word you should record it in your spelling log and find out its definition.

You could set out your spelling log like this:

Word	Definition
appropriate	suitable
autobiography	
basis	
centre	

▶ Record the words in alphabetical order, as this will help you to find the correct word more quickly when you are checking your spelling.

When it comes to learning spellings, practice makes perfect.

▶ Spend time each day checking the words in your spelling log and testing yourself to see if you have learned them correctly.

Here are three techniques that you can use to improve your spelling:

1 Highlight the difficult parts of the word

Often people have problems with a particular part of a word.

▶ To learn the right spelling, write the word on a card, making the difficult part a different colour to the rest of the word.

When you are practising the spelling of the word, picture the card in your mind and read it aloud. When you get to the hard part, think about what it looks and sounds like.

Example

separate.

2 Use a tape recorder to test yourself

Read the words that you are learning into a tape recorder to create your own spelling test.

▶ Say the word.

▶ Give an example of a sentence that uses the word.

▶ Repeat the word.

You can then test yourself whenever you want. Make sure that you pronounce each word correctly and give a sensible example.

Example

Separate. Move to separate desks. Separate.

3 Use the word in a short phrase

Think of different phrases which contain the word and write them out.

Example

We travelled in separate cars.

I am going to separate you two if you cause any more trouble.

This match should separate the best from the rest.

▶ Try to include the words that you are learning in your writing.

By thinking about the spelling of the word when you use it, you are more likely to get it right.

Places

Imaginative writing often involves telling a story. The author creates a picture of a situation in the reader's mind by building up a series of little details. You are going to read an extract from a story set in England during the Second World War. Carrie and Nick have been evacuated to live in the country with Mr Evans and his sister, Miss Evans. Here, Carrie and Nick are visiting Mr Evans's other sister who lives nearby, but to get there they have to go through a dark wood.

T Text level: reading

Pre-reading

How do you think Carrie and Nick might feel about going through the wood? What might they find strange or scary? Read the extract to see if you're right.

Creating a mood

The author, Nina Bawden, makes us feel that something frightening is about to happen by leaving little clues that Carrie and Nick are about to experience something really scary. The clues focus on:

- Carrie's changing feelings throughout the passage
- how the setting becomes increasingly scary.

1 Pick out the words or phrases from the extract that show how Carrie is feeling. Then find the words and phrases that describe the setting.

Carrie's feelings	Setting
Carrie felt a little less bold	*dusk; stars were pricking out in the cold sky above them*

2 How do the words and phrases used to describe the setting make you feel about the woods? Which words make you worry about what will happen to Carrie and Nick?

3 What do you think will happen next? Discuss with a partner what the 'nameless thing' could be and then write down your ideas.

Carrie's War

But when they reached the grove, Carrie felt a little less bold. It was growing dusk; stars were pricking out in the cold sky above them. And it was so quiet, suddenly, that their ears seemed to be singing.

Carrie whispered, 'There's the path down. By that stone.'

Nick's pale face glimmered as he looked up at her. He whispered back, 'You go. I'll wait here.'

'Don't be silly.' Carrie swallowed – then pleaded with him. 'Don't you want a nice mince pie? We might get a mince pie. And it's not far. Auntie Lou said it wasn't far down the hill. Not much more than five minutes.'

Nick shook his head. He screwed up his eyes and put his hands over his ears.

Carrie said coldly, 'All right, have it your own way. But it'll be dark soon and you'll really be scared then. Much more scared by yourself than you would be with me. Druids and ghosts coming to get you! Wild animals too – you don't know! I wouldn't be surprised if there were wolves in these mountains. But I don't care. Even if I hear them howling and snapping their jaws I shan't hurry!'

And she marched off without looking back. White stones marked the path through the yew trees and in the steep places there were steps cut in the earth and shored up with wood. She hadn't gone far when she heard Nick wailing behind her, 'Carrie, wait for me, wait …' She stopped and he skidded into her back. 'Don't leave me, Carrie!'

'I thought it was you leaving me,' she said, making a joke of it, to comfort him, and he tried to laugh but it turned into a tearful sob in his throat.

He hung on to the back of her coat, whimpering under his breath as she led the way down the path. The yew trees grew densely, some of them covered with ivy that rustled and rattled. Like scales, Carrie thought; the trees were like live creatures with scales. She told herself not to be stupid, but stopped to draw breath. She said, 'Do be quiet, Nick.'

'Why?'

'I don't know,' Carrie said. 'Something …'

She couldn't explain it. It was such a strange feeling. As if there was something here, something waiting. Deep in the trees or deep in the earth. Not a ghost – nothing so simple. Whatever it was it had no name. Something old and huge and nameless, Carrie thought, and started to tremble.

Nick said, 'Carrie …'

'Listen.'

'What for?'

'Sssh …'

No sound at first. Then she heard it. A kind of slow, dry whisper, or sigh. As if the earth were turning in its sleep. Or the huge, nameless thing was breathing.

From *Carrie's War* by Nina Bawden

W Word level

Suffixes

A **suffix** is a word ending that is added to the end of a word to make a new word.

Word		Suffix		New word
sigh	+	**ed**	=	sighed
cold	+	**ly**	=	coldly
sigh	+	**ing**	=	sighing
hope	+	**ful**	=	hopeful

When words like 'tip' or 'skim' have a suffix added to them a spelling change takes place. The consonant at the end of the word is doubled before the suffix is added. This only happens when there is a vowel immediately before the consonant at the end of the word.

Word		Suffix		New word
tip	+	**ed**	=	tipped
tip	+	**ing**	=	tipping
skim	+	**ed**	=	skimmed
skim	+	**ing**	=	skimming

1 How many examples of suffixes can you find in the extract?

2 Find three words from the extract that follow the doubled consonant rule.

S Sentence level

Speech punctuation and presentation

When characters speak, the author needs to make it clear to the reader who is speaking. The author does this in several ways:

▶ beginning a **new line** for each new speaker, indented from the margin like a new paragraph

▶ putting everything that the person says in between **speech marks** (' ')

▶ beginning the first word contained in speech marks with a **capital letter** usually

▶ putting a **punctuation mark** before closing the speech marks. This can be a question mark, an exclamation mark, a comma if the speaker is named after the speech, or a full stop

▶ if the speaker is named before the speech, putting a **comma** before the first speech mark.

1 Look at the following passage and pick out the speech punctuation rules that the author uses.

> She told herself not to be stupid, but stopped to draw breath. She said, 'Do be quiet, Nick.'
> 'Why?'
> 'I don't know,' Carrie said. 'Something ...'

2 Now copy out the following passage and replace the * symbol with the correct speech punctuation. Don't look back at the text.

> Carrie whispered * * There's the path down. By that stone * * Nick's pale face glimmered as he looked up at her. He whispered back * * You go. I'll wait here * * Don't be silly.

Retelling a story

You have been asked to retell the story to a class of primary school children. Work with a partner.

▶ Remind yourself of the key features of what happens in the extract on page 17 by making notes.

▶ Use the same techniques as Nina Bawden to keep the reader interested, such as building up little details about the setting and the characters' feelings.

▶ Try it out in front of the class.

Writing to imagine

The extract from *Carrie's War* shows us three of the four important elements that help to create an effective episode from a story:

▶ the **setting** is described and the **characters** are introduced

↓

▶ a **problem** is introduced – they need to get through the frightening wood

↓

▶ the problem reaches a **climax** – when they hear the scary noises.

The fourth most important element is the **resolution**, when the problem is dealt with satisfactorily. You provided your own resolution to this episode when you predicted what would happen next in your answer to question 3 on page 16.

You are now going to write an episode from a story of your own. The writing frame below may be useful to you in helping you to think about the structure your episode should follow.

1 Scene

- Think about where your story is taking place.
- Now think about when your story is taking place.
- Is it inside or outside? In the country or town?
- Is it day or night?
- Is there bright sunshine or is it raining?
- Introduce the characters.
- Where are they when we first see them?
- What are they saying and doing?

2 Problem

- What are the characters trying to do?
- What difficulties or problems could they meet?

3 Climax

- What happens when the problem comes to a head?
- How could you build up to an exciting moment?

4 Resolution

- How is the problem resolved?
- Do things go right in the end or does the story finish unhappily?

Help box

Remember to use words and phrases that help the reader to imagine what is happening.

Places

Unit 3: Explore

People who keep diaries and journals are making a record of the things that they see and hear. These forms of writing allow them **to explore** their reactions to the events that happen to them, as well as to record their feelings. You are going to read an extract from the diary of Samuel Pepys, a public official who lived in London in the seventeenth century. Here he is describing the Great Fire of London, which broke out in September 1666 and destroyed large parts of the city.

Pre-reading

Have you ever kept a journal or a diary? If so, what kind of things did you put in it?

Identifying the main events

1 In the first paragraph of this extract, Pepys writes about how he wasn't worried about the fire at first. Why is this? What finally makes him go to investigate the fire?

2 In the second paragraph, Pepys describes the effect the fire has on people and wildlife. Pick out the words and phrases he uses to make this description dramatic.

3 In the third paragraph, Pepys tells us that nobody seems to be doing anything about the fire. Who does he visit because of this? What do they tell him to do?

4 In the last paragraph, Pepys meets the Lord Mayor. What does the Lord Mayor say he has been doing? How does the description of the Lord Mayor make you feel about him?

The Great Fire of London: the diary of Samuel Pepys

Jane called up about three in the morning, to tell us of a great fire they saw in the City. So I rose, and slipped on my night-gown and went to her window, and thought it to be on the back side of Mark Lane at the farthest; but, being unused to such fires as followed, I thought it far enough off, and so went to bed again, and to sleep... By and by Jane comes and tells me that she hears that above 300 houses have been burned down tonight by the fire we saw, and that it is now burning down all Fish Street, by London Bridge. So I made myself ready presently, and walked to the Tower; and there got up upon one of the high places... and there I did see the houses at the end of the bridge all on fire, and an infinite great fire on this and the other side... of the bridge...

So down [I went], with my heart full of trouble, to the Lieutenant of the Tower, who tells me that it began this morning in the King's baker's house in Pudding Lane, and that it hath burned St Magnus's Church and most part of Fish Street already. So I rode down to the waterside,... and there saw a lamentable fire... Everybody endeavouring to remove their goods, and flinging into the river or bringing them into lighters that lay off; poor people staying in their houses as long as till the very fire touched them, and then running into boats, or clambering from one pair of stairs by the waterside to another. And among other things, the poor pigeons, I perceive, were loth to leave their houses, but hovered about the windows and balconies, till they some of them burned their wings and fell down.

Having stayed, and in an hour's time seen the fire rage every way, and nobody to my sight endeavouring to quench it,... I [went next] to Whitehall (with a gentleman with me, who desired to go off from the Tower to see the fire in my boat); and there up to the King's closet in the Chapel, where people came about me, and I did give them an account [that] dismayed them all, and the word was carried into the King. So I was called for, and did tell the King and Duke of York what I saw; and that unless His Majesty did command houses to be pulled down, nothing could stop the fire. They seemed much troubled, and the King commanded me to go to my Lord Mayor from him, and command him to spare no houses...

[I hurried] to [St] Paul's; and there walked along Watling Street, as well as I could, every creature coming away laden with goods to save and, here and there, sick people carried away in beds. Extraordinary goods carried in carts and on backs. At last [I] met my Lord Mayor in Cannon Street, like a man spent, with a [handkerchief] about his neck. To the King's message he cried, like a fainting woman, 'Lord, what can I do? I am spent: people will not obey me. I have been pulling down houses, but the fire overtakes us faster than we can do it.'...

From *The Diary of Samuel Pepys*

Dictionary check

infinite never-ending
hath has
lamentable distressing
endeavouring trying
lighters flat-bottomed boats
quench stop burning
laden carrying a heavy load
spent exhausted

Prefixes

A **prefix** is a special word beginning that is added to the start of a word to make a new word.

Prefix		Word		New word
dis	+	*like*	=	*dislike*
un	+	*happy*	=	*unhappy*
re	+	*direct*	=	*redirect*
de	+	*rail*	=	*derail*

Sometimes prefixes are used to change the meaning of a word to its opposite, such as 'dislike' and 'unhappy'. However you can only add prefixes to certain words, so you can be 'unpleasant' to somebody, but you can't be 'unnasty'!

There are many types of prefixes, and many of these prefixes have been added to words that are no longer in use today.

1 Copy out and complete the grid below by picking out the words with a prefix from the extract. Then add as many words as you can think of which also use the same prefix.

Prefix	Words in the extract	Other words
in *un* *re* *an* *no* *extra* *over*	*infinite* *unused*	*invite, insight, insane*

Simple sentences

We need to know how words work in sentences and the rules that writers follow when using them. This can help to improve our own writing and make sure that we express our ideas clearly. Here are the basics:

▶ Sentences often describe somebody or something **(noun)** performing an action **(verb)**, sometimes to somebody or something else **(noun)**.

When we put these different parts together in a sentence they are given new names:

▶ The person or thing performing the action is called the **subject** and usually comes at the start of a sentence.

▶ The person or thing receiving the action is called the **object** and usually comes at the end of the sentence.

▶ The **verb** goes in between the subject and object and isn't given another name.

Subject (noun)	Verb	Object (noun)
Man Utd	win	
Jenny	likes	Christian
The dog	bit	the boy

A sentence that is made up of just a subject and a verb or a subject, verb and an object is called a **simple sentence**.

1 Pick subjects, objects and verbs from the table below to create five simple sentences of your own. Make sure that the sentences are believable.

Subject	Verb	Object
the king *the mayor* *everybody* *Jane* *Samuel Pepys*	*wrote* *cried* *saw* *moved* *commanded*	*the mayor* *the fire* *a diary* *their belongings*

2 There are no simple sentences in the Pepys passage at all. Pick out two of his longer sentences and say:

- what is happening in each sentence
- how Pepys makes the sentence dramatic.

SL Speaking and listening

News reporting from 1666

1 Working in a group of four, you are going to perform a role-play. You are interviewing people as they attempt to leave London after the fire begins to spread. You can have any combination of reporters and interviewees, but everyone in your group must get a turn at being a reporter for part of the time. As a reporter, some things you may want to know will be:

▶ What have people heard about the fire?

▶ Has anybody lost a relative or know of anyone who has died?

▶ How do people feel about having to leave their homes, work, friends?

▶ Where are people going to go?

▶ How do they think the people in charge have handled the fire?

You may think of other questions to ask. Also, be prepared to ask further questions when your first questions are answered.

When you have practised your role-play enough times, ask your teacher if you can perform it for the class.

2 Has this role-play helped you to understand people's thoughts and feelings at this time in history? Write brief notes to record what you have learned. Think about:

- ▶ how the people would have reacted to the fire
- ▶ what they would have to do after the fire
- ▶ how you feel about their situation.

Writing to explore

1 You are now going to write a journal or diary entry for a day when an important event took place in your life. It might be your first day at school, moving house, or a time when you did something special.

Use the planning frame below to remind yourself about the important event.

Where did the event happen?

What did you see and hear?

What did you think about the event?

What were your feelings at the time?

Why was the event so important to you?

When you write your journal or diary entry include lots of personal thoughts and feelings. Use the writing frame below to help you.

▶ Today an important event took place when ...

▶ The place where it happened was ...

▶ The first thing I saw was ...

▶ I remember hearing ...

▶ I thought at the time ...

▶ When it was happening I felt ...

▶ I realise that this was an important event because ...

Help box

1 Think about the words you could use to create a vivid picture of the event in the reader's mind.

2 Remember to use the first person 'I' and the past tense 'was', 'felt', 'met'.

Places

Many forms of writing, including stories, poems and plays, can be **entertaining**. The humour in a situation can often come about because of a misunderstanding between two or more people. Here is a scene from the television comedy series *The Two Ronnies* when one of the characters repeatedly misunderstands what the other is saying. This is because the words he uses sound like other words.

Pre-reading

Have you ever said or heard something funny because it has been misunderstood? Was the confusion cleared up in the end?

Working out meaning

Readers and listeners can often work out the meaning of what they are reading or listening to by thinking about the situation. As this scene is set in a hardware shop the situation gives the shopkeeper and the listener certain clues about what the customer means. For instance, because the shop sells candles, when the customer asks for fork handles the shopkeeper gives him four candles! Misunderstandings often occur if the situation gives more than one clue to the meaning of a word or phrase.

1 Copy out and complete the table by picking out all the words that are misunderstood in the scene. Explain why each one is misunderstood. The first one has been done for you.

Misunderstood words	Why?
fork handles	*sounds like 'four candles'*

2 Are there any other reasons why this scene is funny? Discuss your ideas with a partner and then write them down.

The Two Ronnies

In a hardware shop. The shopkeeper is behind the counter, wearing a warehouse jacket. He has just finished serving a customer.

SHOPKEEPER: *(muttering)* There you are. Mind how you go.

Another customer enters the shop, wearing a scruffy tank top and beanie.

CUSTOMER: Fork handles!

SHOPKEEPER: Four candles?

CUSTOMER: Fork handles.

(The shopkeeper makes for a box, and gets out four candles. He places them on the counter)

CUSTOMER: No, fork handles!

SHOPKEEPER: *(confused)* Well, there you are – four candles!

CUSTOMER: No, fork 'andles! 'Andles for forks!

(The shopkeeper puts the candles away, and goes to get a fork handle. He places it onto the counter)

SHOPKEEPER: *(muttering)* Fork handles. Thought you said 'four candles'!

(more clearly) Next?

CUSTOMER: Got any plugs?

SHOPKEEPER: Plugs. What kind of plugs?

CUSTOMER: A rubber one, bathroom.

(The shopkeeper gets out a box of bath plugs, and places it on the counter)

SHOPKEEPER: *(pulling out two different sized plugs)* What size?

CUSTOMER: Thirteen amp!

SHOPKEEPER: *(muttering)* It's electric bathroom plugs, we call them, in the trade Electric bathroom plugs!

(He puts the box away, gets out another box, and places an electric plug on the counter and then puts the box away)

CUSTOMER: Saw tips!

SHOPKEEPER: Saw tips? *(He doesn't know what he means)* What d'you want? Ointment, or something like that?

CUSTOMER: No, saw tips for covering saws.

SHOPKEEPER: Oh, haven't got any, haven't got any. *(He mutters)* Comin' in, but we haven' got any. Next?

CUSTOMER: 'O's!

SHOPKEEPER: Hoes?

CUSTOMER: 'O's.

(He goes to get a hoe, and places it on the counter)

CUSTOMER: No, 'O's!

SHOPKEEPER: Hose! I thought you said 'hoes!' *(He takes the hoe back, and gets a hose, whilst muttering)* When you said 'hose', I thought you said 'hoes!' Hose!

(He places the hose onto the counter)

CUSTOMER: No, 'O's!

SHOPKEEPER: *(confused for a moment)* O's? Oh, you mean panty 'hose', panty 'hose'. He picks up a pair of tights from beside him)

CUSTOMER: No, no, 'O's! 'O's — for the gate. 'O's! Letter 'O's!

SHOPKEEPER: *(finally realising):* Letter O's! *(muttering)* You had me going there!

(He climbs up a stepladder, gets a box down, puts the ladder away, and takes the box to the counter, and searches through it for letter 'O's)

SHOPKEEPER: How many d'you want?

CUSTOMER: Two.

(The shopkeeper leaves two letter 'O's on the counter, then takes the box back, gets the ladder out again, puts the box away, climbs down the ladder, and puts the ladder away, then returns to the counter)

SHOPKEEPER: Yes, next?

CUSTOMER: Got any 'P's?

From *All I Ever Wrote* by Ronnie Barker

 Word level

Homophones

Two words that sound the same but are spelt differently are called **homophones**.

Hoes Hose	*sound alike*

There Their They're	*sound alike*

1 Copy out the table and replace the pictures with the right word.

there	their
your	you're
week	weak
here	hear
past	passed
allowed	aloud

weather	whether
male	
right	
meat	
bare	
feat	

2 Copy out and complete the following passage using some of the homophones from the above table.

Last _____ after school I went to the hardware shop. I met my friend, Aaron on the way _____. He wasn't _____ out really because he hadn't done his homework. We both turned _____ into the shop and asked the manager _____ he had any enamel paint for a model airplane I was making. 'Enamel paint,' shouted the man, '_____ joking! I haven't had that _____ for years!' We left the shop very disappointed.

Unclear sentences

Misunderstandings can happen easily when sentences are confusingly written.

1 Look at the following sentences and decide why they are unclear. Match them up with the correct reason. One is done for you.

Unclear sentence	Reason for being unclear
1 I have a cat with one leg called Tiddles. 2 Only guide dogs are allowed here. 3 She took the pencil out of her pencil case and sharpened it. 4 She didn't hurt nobody.	a using the word 'only' b using negatives twice c careless word order d confusing use of pronoun

2 Look at the following sentences and explain why each one is unclear.

a) Wanted! Basket for dog with a solid bottom.

b) Only wear trainers in the sports hall.

c) He took his dirty football jersey out of his sports bag and threw it into the washing machine.

d) I didn't say nothing.

3 Now rewrite the sentences from questions 1 and 2 so that they become clear.

SL Speaking and listening

Performing a script

With a partner you are going to perform the script from *The Two Ronnies*. First you have to plan how you and your partner are going to act out the lines. Think about the ways you could make the scene funny. Follow this directing frame to help you plan your performance.

Voice	Shopkeeper	Customer
What kind of accent would the characters have — rough, posh or from a particular part of the country?		

Attitude	Shopkeeper	Customer
How would he show his feelings?		
How would he react?		
How does he explain things — slowly, impatiently?		

Behaviour	Shopkeeper	Customer
How would he act — rushed, eager to help?		
How does he explain things — slowly, impatiently?		

Key parts of the scene	Shopkeeper	Customer
In which parts of the scene are words misunderstood? Remember these words and the reasons why they are misunderstood.		

You are now ready to act the scene out. Follow this plan.

▶ Decide which part you want to play.

▶ Read over the scene at least twice with your partner.

▶ Remind yourselves of the key parts of the scene.

▶ Do not worry if you cannot remember all the other words in the scene – a rough guess at the unimportant words will do.

When you are confident that you have something funny to show the rest of the class, you can ask your teacher if you can present your work.

Writing to entertain

You are now going to write your own humorous script. Base it on a misunderstanding between two or more people. It might be about:

▶ what someone thought the other person had said

▶ what someone thought the other person did.

Remind yourself about commonly confused words by looking back at the section on homophones on page 34. Think about situations where these words could cause confusion, for example a conversation between two school friends, a parent talking to their child, two people meeting for the first time. Use the writing frame on page 38 to help you work out what will happen.

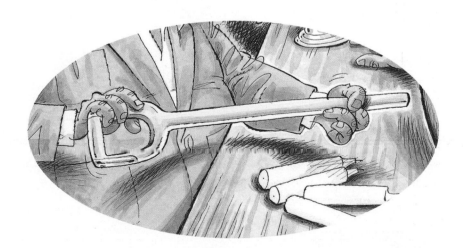

Setting

Where and when does the misunderstanding take place?

Characters

Are they friends, family or strangers?

Situation

What is the misunderstanding about?

First character

What does the first person say or do?

Second character

What does the other person think the first person said or did?

Reactions

How do both the characters react?

Consequences

What happens because of the misunderstanding?

Help box

Don't forget to present your writing as a play script and try to make it funny.

Reading log ▶▶▶

Keeping a reading log is a good way of keeping track of the books you have read. This can help you to identify the types of books that you enjoy, as well as making a note of any authors whose books you like. Whilst you are reading a book, a reading log allows you to make a record of the chapters that you have read and also encourages you to think about what might happen in the next part of the book.

▶ Start your reading log by completing the details for the three texts that you have read in this section: the extract from *Carrie's War*, Samuel Pepys' diary and *The Two Ronnies* sketch.

After you have filled in this section of the reading log, you could look for other books by the authors that you have read in this section, or books with similar themes. Set out the reading log like the one below:

Title *Carrie's War*	**Author** Nina Bawden

Plot

It is about two children who are evacuated to the countryside during the Second World War.

What's happening in the story

Carrie and Nick are going through the dark woods. Nick doesn't want to go but Carrie encourages him. They both get scared when they hear a strange noise.

Prediction

I think that the noise will turn out to be a harmless animal and they will both feel silly for being so frightened.

Rating

8/10 – a tense and exciting part of the story.

▶ You should fill in your reading log each time you read your book. When you have completed your reading log, make a poster promoting your favourite books and encouraging other people to read them. You could also make a list of your top ten favourite books.

Round the class story ▶▶▶

You are going to take part in creating a story about three children who have gone on an adventure holiday together to the Cornish coast. Here is the beginning of the story.

> Sam, Billy and Mel were looking forward to the first day of their adventure holiday. Unfortunately, when they woke up on the first morning of their holiday they were told that nobody was free to take them white-water rafting. They were all very disappointed. However ...

Each member of the class will take a turn to continue the story and must use at least one word or phrase from any of the boxes 1 to 3, before handing on the story to the next pupil by using a phrase from box 4. Try to keep the story interesting and exciting and see how many times you can take it round the class.

wonderful	fearfully	replied	however
marvellous	hesitantly	answered	after this
incredible	joyfully	responded	a result of this
fantastic	sadly	retorted	consequently
exciting	gradually	whispered	nevertheless
thrilling	constantly	shouted	then
frightening	consistently	snapped	so
petrifying	unusually	giggled	yet
worrying	rarely	chuckled	but
	uncertainly		

Make a note of the words or phrases from the boxes that you have used when taking your turn to tell the story. Try to use as many as you can, but make sure that the story still makes sense.

Travel

Informative writing is all about giving readers the correct information about a topic or activity to help them understand it. People who write instructions go a little further and tell readers how to perform the activity. You are going to read a leaflet that gives information about how to cycle safely.

T Text level: reading

Pre-reading

What do you think are the most important things to remember about safety when cycling? Can you think of any special equipment that cyclists use?

Identifying how the main points are presented

1 Why can cycling be a dangerous hobby?

2 What does the law say cyclists should have on their bikes?

3 Where on the road should cyclists take special care?

4 How will the police help you with bike security?

5 How does the writer present the information in a helpful way for young cyclists? Think about the way the writer uses layout and images.

Cycling know-how

Cycling is both a relaxing and enjoyable hobby, but due to the increased traffic on our roads, cycling can sometimes be dangerous.

Be seen to be safe

The right clothes can help you to be seen – fluorescent clothing during the day, reflective clothing at night. The law says you must use front and rear lights and a red rear reflector at night, so make sure that they're clean and working properly. If you have an accident, a cycle helmet can help to prevent a serious injury to your head. Make sure your helmet is the right size and is properly fitted. As a rule, you should just be able to see the rim of the helmet above your eyes when it is on.

Look after your bike

Before you go cycling, you should always carefully check your bike. Look over moving parts often, giving special attention to brakes and lights. Make sure that your tyres are properly inflated and that you can see the tread on them clearly. They need frequent inspection for damage. Your wheels should spin freely without rubbing against the brakes and should not wobble.

On the road

Be alert and always look around before starting your journey. Use side streets to avoid very busy roads if you can. Wherever one road joins another, you should take great care – this is especially true at roundabouts. Clear hand signals are always very important, and remember to watch out for careless drivers cutting in front of you. Always check that it is safe before joining a main road – if it's not, stop! If a situation looks tricky, get off your bike and walk it along the pavement to a safe crossing point.

Bike security

When securing your bike it's best to use a lock rather than chains, as chains can be easily cut with strong bolt cutters or hacksaws. You can now buy cycle alarms as well, but don't get a vibration sensitive alarm as the smallest gust of wind sets most of them off! Contact your local police station and ask them about bike stamping. Most police stations provide this service free of charge and it can help them to track down your bike if it ever goes missing. Finally, you should also get your bike insured. This can be arranged through insurance brokers, cycling clubs or bike shops.

Remember! Cycling is fun if you stay on the right track.

Dictionary check

fluorescent day-glow
inflated blown up with air
inspection check
vibration gentle movement

From Our Guide to Safe On-Road Cycling

Words used to qualify ideas

In the leaflet the word 'carefully' is used to describe the way cyclists should check their bikes before setting out. The word 'carefully' is an example of an **adverb**.

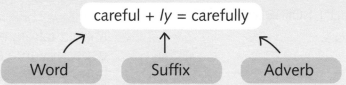

careful + *ly* = carefully

Word   Suffix   Adverb

The suffix (-ly) is added to the word (careful) to make a new word (carefully). There are other examples of 'ly' words that are adverbs in the passage.

1 Copy out and complete the table below by picking out adverbs from the passage that end with the suffix 'ly'. Try to say what the adverb does in the sentence. The first one has been done for you.

Adverb	Word	What the adverb does
carefully	*careful*	*describes the action of checking the bike*

The writer also uses words to describe nouns. These describing words are called **adjectives.**

relaxing + hobby = relaxing hobby

Adjective   Noun

2 Pick out the adjectives you can find in the passage. For each one, explain the effect that the adjective has on the noun.

Phrases and expanding sentences

The writers of information texts always try to give the reader precise information.

> *The writer could have written:*
> Chains can be cut with bolt cutters.
>
> *The writer actually wrote:*
> Chains can be easily cut with strong bolt cutters.

The adverb 'easily' extends the part of the sentence about the action of cutting and the adjective 'strong' extends the part of the sentence about the bolt cutters. When a group of words makes up a single part of a sentence, it's called a **phrase**. We could have extended the 'chains' part of the sentence by adding extra information as below.

Phrase	Phrase	**Phrase**

Metal bicycle chains can be easily cut **with strong bolt cutters.**

Using phrases is a helpful way of giving the reader extra information.

1 Copy out the following sentences and pick out the separate phrases using different colours. The first one has been done for you.

   a) Mountain bikes should be carefully checked for brake damage.

   b) Fluorescent clothing is clearly visible on dark nights.

   c) The safe cyclist always notices careless drivers.

   d) Clear hand signals are very important.

   e) Your local police station should provide a bike stamping service.

2 Expand the phrases in the following sentences by adding extra information. The first one has been done for you.

a) The boy crossed the road.

> Example
>
> *The young boy carefully crossed the busy road.*

b) Cycling is a hobby.
c) A helmet protects the head from injury.
d) Drivers can cause accidents.
e) Breezes set off alarms.

SL Speaking and listening

Giving clear instructions

Look at the following instructions that tell you how to repair a punctured tyre on a bike. With a partner, work out the correct order of the instructions. The first one has been done for you.

Instruction 1 = c)

---

a) When you have applied the glue let it sit for about 3–5 minutes. Then peel the foil off the patch and press it onto the glue.

b) First of all you need to turn the bike upside down and stand it on its seat and handlebars. This allows you to take off the wheel easily.

c) I am going to tell you how to fix a flat tyre on a bike. To do this you need an air pump, plastic tyre levers and a bicycle patch kit.

d) Next, pull the inner-tube completely out of the tyre. Pump up the inner-tube and pass it slowly in front of your face. You should be able to hear or feel the hissing of air out of the tube. Once you find the leak, deflate the inner-tube and prepare to patch it.

e) Using the tyre levers, pop one side of the tyre off the rim so that you can see the inner-tube.

f) Finally, let the patch dry for a couple of minutes before reinstalling the tube and putting the tyre back on the wheel.

g) The area that is to be patched needs to be cleaned. If you are using glue, sand down the area to be patched before applying the glue.

h) Once the wheel is off, use the tyre levers to remove the tyre. Make sure the inner-tube is fully deflated and using your thumbs, push the tyre away from the rim and insert the tyre levers.

When you have decided the correct order of the instructions, practise presenting them in your pair. Remember to think about:

- presenting the instructions clearly and at a suitable pace
- the importance of emphasising key points
- using a whiteboard or diagram to help to point out important instructions.

Writing to inform

In the leaflet the writer is informing us about the hobby of cycling. You are now going to write to inform a reader of your own age about a hobby you have. It might be information about:

- a sport you play
- a club you belong to
- an activity you really enjoy.

You must present the information clearly, in an organised way. Start by brainstorming the task. This planning frame may help.

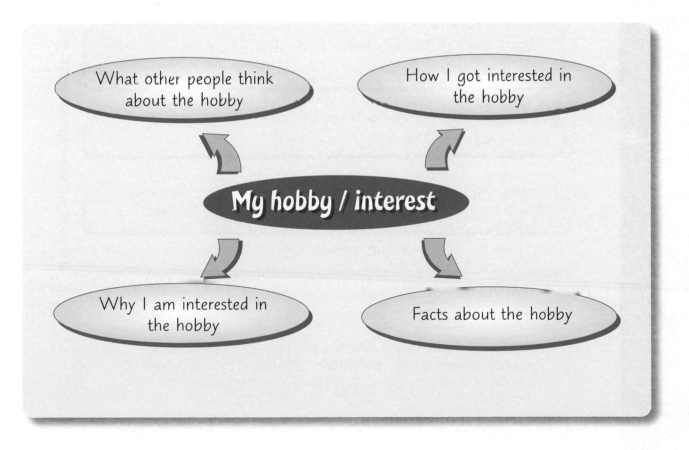

This writing frame may be useful in helping you to structure your informative writing:

1 In this essay I am going to inform you about my hobby. It is ...

2 The first thing I would like to tell you about is how I got interested in my hobby. This was because ...

3 There are several aspects of the hobby I would like to tell you about. These are ...

4 I really like this hobby because ...

5 Next I want to tell you about some facts. These are ...
This is interesting because ...

6 Finally, other people think my hobby is ...

7 The reason I am still interested in this hobby is because ...

Help box

1. The following adverbs and adjectives may be useful in your writing.
   Adverbs: cleverly, skilfully, wonderfully, brilliantly, marvellously, adeptly.
   Adjectives: exciting, captivating, fascinating, thrilling, absorbing, fantastic.

2. You might want to use sub-headings and pictures to make the information clear for the reader.

Travel

Unit 6: Explain

Explaining involves looking closely at how something works or showing why something has happened. An effective explanation should help readers to understand more about something that they did not know about, by presenting ideas in a clear and straightforward way. You are going to look at a website about how hot-air balloons fly.

Pre-reading

Have you ever seen a hot-air balloon in the sky? Ever wondered how they are controlled so accurately to take off and land?

Finding information

Skim-read the article to find the answers to the following questions.

1 What are the three major parts of a hot-air balloon?

2 How does the balloon rise and descend?

3 Once in the air, how does the balloon change direction?

4 What does the 'chase crew' do?

5 Copy out and complete the grid below. Pick out the different examples the writer uses to make his or her explanation clear and say what each example shows. The first one has been done for you.

Example	What it shows
freezer	*how hot air rises and cold air sinks*

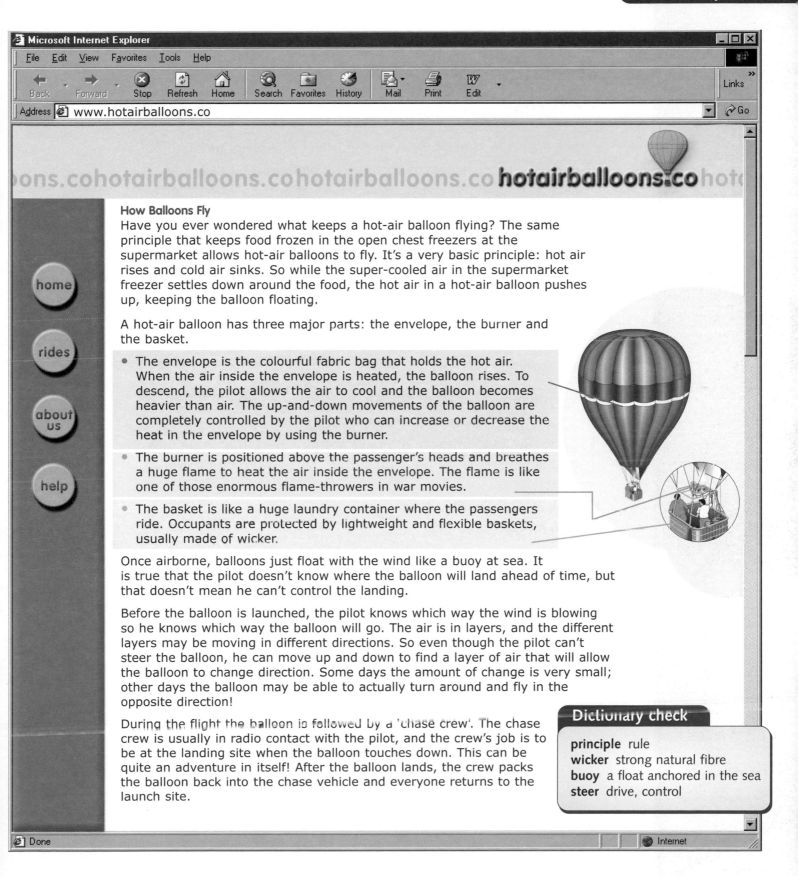

How Balloons Fly

Have you ever wondered what keeps a hot-air balloon flying? The same principle that keeps food frozen in the open chest freezers at the supermarket allows hot-air balloons to fly. It's a very basic principle: hot air rises and cold air sinks. So while the super-cooled air in the supermarket freezer settles down around the food, the hot air in a hot-air balloon pushes up, keeping the balloon floating.

A hot-air balloon has three major parts: the envelope, the burner and the basket.

- The envelope is the colourful fabric bag that holds the hot air. When the air inside the envelope is heated, the balloon rises. To descend, the pilot allows the air to cool and the balloon becomes heavier than air. The up-and-down movements of the balloon are completely controlled by the pilot who can increase or decrease the heat in the envelope by using the burner.

- The burner is positioned above the passenger's heads and breathes a huge flame to heat the air inside the envelope. The flame is like one of those enormous flame-throwers in war movies.

- The basket is like a huge laundry container where the passengers ride. Occupants are protected by lightweight and flexible baskets, usually made of wicker.

Once airborne, balloons just float with the wind like a buoy at sea. It is true that the pilot doesn't know where the balloon will land ahead of time, but that doesn't mean he can't control the landing.

Before the balloon is launched, the pilot knows which way the wind is blowing so he knows which way the balloon will go. The air is in layers, and the different layers may be moving in different directions. So even though the pilot can't steer the balloon, he can move up and down to find a layer of air that will allow the balloon to change direction. Some days the amount of change is very small; other days the balloon may be able to actually turn around and fly in the opposite direction!

During the flight the balloon is followed by a 'chase crew'. The chase crew is usually in radio contact with the pilot, and the crew's job is to be at the landing site when the balloon touches down. This can be quite an adventure in itself! After the balloon lands, the crew packs the balloon back into the chase vehicle and everyone returns to the launch site.

Dictionary check

principle rule
wicker strong natural fibre
buoy a float anchored in the sea
steer drive, control

Spelling strategies and defining words in context

If we are not sure of the correct spelling of a word or what it means, we can always look it up in a **dictionary.** A dictionary also gives us other helpful information about the word. Lots of words have more than one meaning and we can only tell which is the right one by looking at their context.

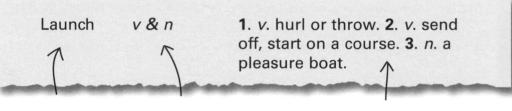

Launch   *v & n*   **1.** *v.* hurl or throw. **2.** *v.* send off, start on a course. **3.** *n.* a pleasure boat.

Headword   **Part of speech**   **Definitions**

1 Copy out and complete the table below. Check that you know how to spell each of the words from the passage by following these steps:

▶ **look** at each word in turn
▶ **cover** it up
▶ **close your eyes** and 'see' the word in your mind's eye, as if it is a picture
▶ **write down** the word in the column below
▶ **check** to see if you got it right
▶ if necessary, **correct** the spelling.

Word	Spelling guess	Correction	Definition

principle   envelope   burner   basket
flexible   descend   flight   balloon

2 Look up the meaning of the words using a dictionary. If a word has more than one meaning, look back at the passage and choose the meaning that fits best. Write each definition in the table.

S Sentence level

Active and passive voice

Most sentences are in the **active voice.** In most sentences the subject comes before the verb. The subject of an active sentence is the person or thing doing the action.

However, in some sentences the emphasis and word order is different. The subject moves to the end of the sentence and becomes the agent. This is called the **passive voice.** Sometimes we can even miss out who does the acting.

Active voice	**The pilot** launched the balloon.
Passive voice	The ballon was launched by **the pilot.**
	The ballon was launched.

The passive voice is a more impersonal style and is often used by the writers of explanation texts.

1 Change the examples of the passive voice into the active voice. The first one has been done for you.

Passive voice	Active voice
Occupants are protected by lightweight and flexible baskets, usually made of wicker.	*Lightweight and flexible baskets, usually made of wicker, protect the occupants.*
The balloon is followed by a chase crew.	*A chase crew …*
The up-and-down movements of the balloon are completely controlled by the pilot.	

2 Copy out these active sentences and change them into the passive voice. What effect does changing them into the passive voice have?

a) Brian Jones and Bertrand Pickard flew a hot-air balloon around the world.

Example

A hot-air balloon …

b) The Montgolfier brothers invented the first hot-air balloon.

c) Many people enjoy the peace and quiet of a balloon flight.

Giving a rehearsed talk

With a partner, plan a speech to be made to the rest of the class explaining how something works. Choose a topic that you are interested in – it could be how a mobile phone sends text messages or how a motor scooter or electric toothbrush works. When you are planning your speech follow these steps:

• use the Internet to find out information that will help you make the speech

• with your partner, divide the speech into sections that you can each read out

• practise speaking clearly and at an appropriate pace for your audience to understand.

When you are ready, ask your teacher to let you make your speech to the rest of the class.

Writing to explain

In the article, the writer explains how a hot-air balloon flies. You are now going to write an explanation about how something that you know about works. It might be:

• a favourite model, toy or item of sports equipment

• a form of transport, like a motorbike or scooter

• a gadget or machine that you own, such as a gameboy.

Your audience is a person of your own age who has very little knowledge of the thing you are writing about. Set out the explanation clearly, giving lots of examples to help the reader to understand.

This writing frame may help.

Opening statement

Tell the reader what you are going to explain.

Step-by-step explanation

Take your reader through the activity stage by stage. Remember to give examples that will help the reader to understand your explanation.

Step 1:

Step 2:

Step 3:

Step 4:

Concluding statement

Sum up for the reader what you have explained.

Help box

1. Words to do with **time** and **cause** are really useful for a piece of writing such as this. See if you can include some or all of these:

After	First	Then	As a result
Next	Following	Finally	

2. Remember to try to use the passive voice because this will help you keep the focus on the thing you are describing.

Travel

Unit 7: Describe

When you are describing a place, person or an object you are using words to paint a picture. Descriptive writing may involve all the senses of sight, touch, smell, sound and taste. The more the writer uses the senses to describe something, the easier it will be for the reader to picture the description. In this passage, taken from the horror story *Dracula*, a frightening coach journey at night through the wild countryside of Transylvania is described.

T Text level: reading

Pre-reading

Have you ever had a frightening journey? What made it scary?

Character and setting

> The person who is telling the story is called the **narrator**. In this passage the writer uses **first person narrative**, where all the details of the story are seen through the eyes of one person. You can usually tell that a story is in the first person if the person telling the story is referred to as 'I'.

1 What reasons does the narrator give for feeling afraid in the first paragraph?

2 In the second paragraph the narrator says something happened that seemed like 'a sort of awful nightmare'? What is this?

3 How does the writer build up the tension in the second and third paragraphs? Think about what he sees and hears.

4 In the last paragraph, what happens to the horses to make the narrator even more fearful? What does the narrator see by the light of the moon?

5 In this extract the reader is made to feel what the narrator feels by the author's use of the senses to describe the journey. For the first paragraph only, fill in the grid below:

What he sees	trees arching over the road
What he hears	
What he feels	

Dracula

Soon we were hemmed in with trees, which in places arched right over the roadway till we passed as through a tunnel. And again great frowning rocks guarded us boldly on either side. Though we were in shelter, we could hear the rising wind, for it moaned and whistled through the rocks, and the branches of the trees crashed together as we swept along. It grew colder and colder still, and fine, powdery snow began to fall, so that soon we and all around us were covered with a white blanket. The keen wind still carried the howling of the dogs, though this grew fainter as we went on our way. The baying of the wolves sounded nearer and nearer, as though they were closing round on us from every side. I grew dreadfully afraid, and the horses shared my fear. The driver, however, was not in the least disturbed. He kept turning his head to left and right, but I could not see anything through the darkness.

Suddenly, away on our left I saw a faint flickering blue flame. The driver saw it at the same moment. He at once checked the horses, and, jumping to the ground, disappeared into the darkness. I did not know what to do, the less as the howling of the wolves grew closer. But while I wondered, the driver suddenly appeared again, and without a word took his seat, and we resumed our journey. I think I must have fallen asleep and kept dreaming of the incident, for it seemed to be repeated endlessly, and now looking back, it is like a sort of awful nightmare. Once the flame appeared so near the road, that even in the darkness around us I could watch the driver's motions. He went rapidly to where the blue flame arose, it must have been very faint, for it did not seem to illumine the place around it at all, and gathering a few stones, formed them into some device.

Once there appeared a strange optical effect. When he stood between me and the flame he did not obstruct it, for I could see its ghostly flicker all the same. This startled me, but as the effect was only momentary, I took it that my eyes deceived me, straining through the darkness. Then for a time there were no blue flames, and we sped onwards through the gloom, with the howling of the wolves around us, as though they were following in a moving circle.

At last there came a time when the driver went further afield than he had yet gone, and during his absence, the horses began to tremble worse than ever and to snort and scream with fright. I could not see any cause for it, for the howling of the wolves had ceased altogether. But just then the moon, sailing through the black clouds, appeared behind the jagged crest of a beetling, pine-clad rock, and by its light I saw around us a ring of wolves, with white teeth and lolling red tongues, with long, sinewy limbs and shaggy hair. They were a hundred times more terrible in the grim silence which held them than even when they howled. For myself, I felt a sort of paralysis of fear. It is only when a man feels himself face to face with such horrors that he can understand their true import.

From *Dracula* by Bram Stoker

Dictionary check

keen sharp
baying howling, crying
illumine light up
beetling overhanging
paralysis state of being unable to move
import meaning

Personification and onomatopoeia

One of the techniques the author, Bram Stoker, uses to help him describe this scene is **personification.** This is where an object is given the qualities of a person.

> the great *frowning* rocks

The word 'frowning' is used to describe the way the rocks appeared to the narrator – as if they were people frowning at him. This makes the rocks seem grim and forbidding.

1 In the table below, there are other examples of personification used in the extract. Can you explain what picture the writer wants us to imagine?

Personification	What the reader imagines
rocks guarded us	
the rising wind, for it moaned and whistled	
the keen wind still carried the howling	
the grim silence	

Another technique Stoker uses is to choose words that closely represent the sounds that the narrator hears.

> ... *the branches of the trees **crashed** together*

The reader can hear the sound in the word 'crashed'. This technique is called **onomatopoeia.**

2 Pick out other examples of onomatopoeia in the passage. Explain what you think the use of onomatopoeia adds to the description.

 Sentence level

Building longer sentences

Writers build up interesting details in their descriptive writing by using longer sentences.

Main event of the sentence

This adds an extra detail by describing what the trees look like

Soon we were hemmed in with trees, which in places arched right over the roadway till we passed as through the tunnel.

Another event happening in the sentence

More extra information describing their passing through the trees

The main event happening in the sentence is the narrator and the driver being 'hemmed in' by the trees. The reader is also told that that they passed through these trees. But the writer adds interest for the reader by adding some more information about the trees and the way the characters passed through the trees.

1 Copy out the sentences below and, by highlighting or underlining, identify:

- the main events happening
- the extra information given in these sentences.

a) Though we were in shelter, we could hear the rising wind, for it moaned and whistled through the rocks, and the branches of the trees crashed together as we swept along.

b) The baying of the wolves sounded nearer and nearer, as though they were closing round on us from either side.

c) But just then the moon, sailing through the black clouds, appeared behind the jagged crest of beetling, pine-clad rock, and by its light I saw around us a ring of wolves, with white teeth and lolling red tongues, with long, sinewy limbs.

d) This startled me, but as the effect was only momentary, I took it that my eyes deceived me straining through the darkness.

2 How do you think these longer sentences add to a reader's enjoyment of the description? Pick out two or three descriptive details from the passage that make the reader really want to read on.

SL Speaking and listening

Asking searching questions

You are going to put the driver from the *Dracula* extract in the 'hot seat'. Work in groups of four. Follow these steps to complete the task.

1 Elect one person in your group to play the role of the driver.

2 Working together, think up as many questions as you can about:
- why he acts the way he does
- his thoughts and feelings about driving the carriage that night
- what he thinks will happen next.

3 Work together on what the answers to these questions might be.

4 Each person playing the driver will then be on the 'hot seat' out in front of the whole class. They will answer the questions prepared by his or her group, after which the whole class will get the opportunity to ask their own questions.

Your group will need to make sure that the person playing the driver is ready to answer any questions that the rest of the class might ask.

Writing to describe

You are now going to write a description of a favourite place that you have. You will want to involve the five senses and could even use techniques such as personification and onomatopoeia. Try to interest the reader by including details that help them to build up a picture of the place you are describing.

You could plan the task using the spider diagram below and thinking about some of the suggestions given.

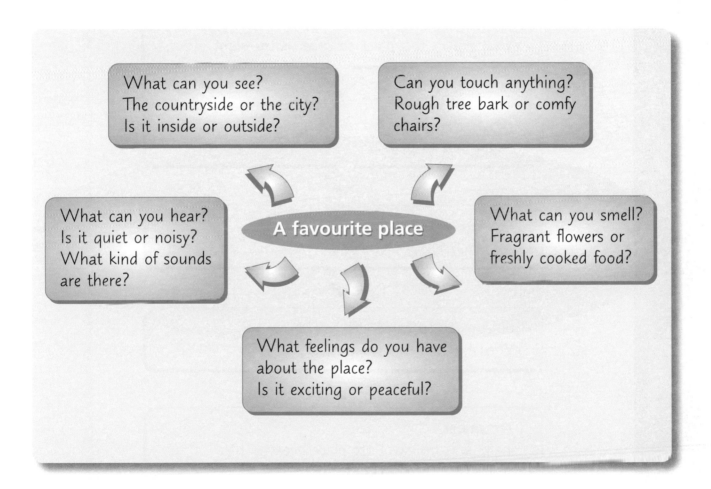

What can you see?
The countryside or the city?
Is it inside or outside?

Can you touch anything?
Rough tree bark or comfy chairs?

What can you hear?
Is it quiet or noisy?
What kind of sounds are there?

A favourite place

What can you smell?
Fragrant flowers or freshly cooked food?

What feelings do you have about the place?
Is it exciting or peaceful?

When you have made your notes you can go on to attempt a continuous piece of writing. This writing frame may help.

I am going to describe my favourite place. It's …
What I like about it is …

↓

Here you can see …
What makes this place so great is the sight of …

↓

I would like to tell you about some of the sounds …
I really love to hear …

↓

There are different smells of …
I especially like the scent of …

↓

Sometimes you can touch …
When I am in this place I feel …

↓

I remember …
Finally, it is my favourite place because …

Help box

Remember to use personification and onomatopoeia and build up a picture of the place you are describing.

Spelling log ▶▶▶

In this section you have read two texts, *Cycling know-how* and *How balloons fly*, that include a lot of specialist vocabulary, such as 'fluorescent'. In addition to this, you have also read an extract from *Dracula*, a novel written in the nineteenth century, which includes archaic words such as 'lolling'.

▶ Look back at the texts that you have read in this section and pick out any words that you are unfamiliar with. Add these words to your spelling log and look up their meanings in a dictionary.

Here are some words that you might want to add to your spelling log:

Word	Definition
colourful	
fainter	
hemmed	
principle	
reflective	
vibration	

You might also want to use a thesaurus to find other words that have a similar meaning.

▶ Map these out in a word-web like the one shown below.

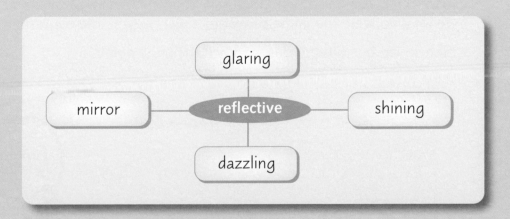

The Literacy Zone ▶▶▶

You and a partner have been chosen to set questions for a quiz show called the Literacy Zone. The questions must all be about the things that you have learned in this section of the book and include questions about:

- ▶ adverbs and adjectives
- ▶ active and passive voice
- ▶ personification and onomatopoeia.

In the Literacy Zone contestants are asked a series of six questions. These questions are worth 10 points, 20 points, 30 points, 40 points, 50 points and 100 points. With your partner discuss and write down six questions to test the contestants. The more points a question is worth, the more difficult it should be.

Here is an example of a Literacy Zone question:

> **What does onomatopoeia mean?**
>
> ▶ A word used to represent the smell of something.
> ▶ A word used to represent the sound of something.
> ▶ A word used to describe a name which has a lot of syllables in it.
> ▶ The sound of a name which has a lot of syllables in it.
> ▶ A word used to show what something looks like.
>
> ?

When you have finished working out the six questions, team up with another pair and run the game. You and your partner will take turns to ask your questions of the other pair. You will then swap over and the team who were the game show hosts will become the contestants.

See which team in the class can win the most points.

Leisure

Unit 8: Persuade

Persuasive writing is about changing people's minds. Words, phrases and sentences are carefully chosen to convince readers that they should think in a certain way. Sometimes pictures and other visual techniques are used as well. You are going to read an advertising feature that uses words, pictures and other devices in an attempt to persuade the reader to go on a cycling weekend.

T Text level: reading

Pre-reading

Do you think advertisements are successful in persuading people to buy things or go to particular places? How might you be persuaded to go on a cycling weekend?

Identifying how texts persuade

1 Where in the UK can you go on a Skedaddle Weekend holiday?

2 What kind of accommodation is offered?

3 What are WOWs?

4 How does the writer try to make the information in the article clear for the reader? Consider the use of columns, headings and sub-headings, and the little icons.

5 What do the pictures show? How might they help to persuade people to go on a Skedaddle Weekend?

6 What sort of information is given down the left-hand side of the page? Why is this information helpful for the reader?

7 Pick out some of the words and phrases that are used in the article to persuade the reader to go on this holiday. Choose three and say why they are persuasive.

> Example
>
> *Fancy two days of **great** biking in the **most beautiful** parts of the UK?*
>
> *Positive language makes the weekend sound fun*

8 What type of cyclist is the advertisement aimed at? Give reasons for your answer.

UK – Skedaddle Weekends
Cycling shorts!

Activity

Biking
2 days
Supported

Tour duration

2 days

Accommodation

Centre based
Converted barn
or B&B
All meals provided

Grade

Beginners	1-2
Derbyshire	2-3
Brecon Beacons	3
Exmoor	3
Yorkshire Dales	3-4
Dorset	3

Price

£125

Dates

SW02/01
Dorset
22 February 2002

SW02/04
Exmoor
12 April 2002

SW02/08
Brecon
28 June 2002

SW02/09
Derbyshire
26 July 2002

SW02/10
Yorkshire
9 August 2002

Fancy two days of great biking in the most beautiful parts of the UK? Then Skedaddle Weekends are for you!

Held throughout the year, Skedaddle Weekends provide the opportunity to explore the hidden corners of the South Downs, Cotswolds, Exmoor, Derbyshire Peak District, Yorkshire Dales and the Brecon Beacons.

These fun short breaks are an excellent way to explore new and exciting parts of the UK, meet the Skedaddle Team for a chat and provide a perfect opportunity to catch up with old friends from previous trips and make new ones.

All rides are fully guided, so no need to look at the map every two minutes, and with our support vehicle close at hand, all you'll need to have with you is your water supply and your favourite chocolate bar – and we'll even provide that!

Mostly off-road, the routes vary in degrees of difficulty. Each is graded although there is a degree of flexibility to cater for the abilities and requirements of the specific group.

Accommodation varies from wonderfully rustic converted barns and rural cottages to Bed and Breakfasts, depending on location.

We pride ourselves on providing great value weekends with no hidden extras. Filling breakfasts, delicious buffet style lunches and tasty evening meals, plus an endless supply of snacks during the ride, ensure no sneaky additional costs.

Beginners / Basic Maintenance Weekends

Specifically designed for those just starting out in mountain biking, these low-level biking weekends offer advice and instruction on riding techniques in a relaxed atmosphere on a variety of carefully selected tracks and trails. The riding is combined with simple advice on the basics of bike maintenance and what to do if things go wrong.

Women Only Weekends

Based around the usual Skedaddle Weekend format and now in their third year, our WOWs are firmly established in the Skedaddle calendar. Designed for those who enjoy mountain biking but prefer doing so in a male free environment, they continue to grow in popularity.

Dictionary check

rustic having a countryside appearance
rural to do with the countryside

W Word level

Word links with different languages

Sometimes it can help our spelling to know where a word comes from in the past. The words in the left-hand column of the table are used in the advertisement. Although they are all English words, they originally come from different languages.

1 Match each English word with the word that it comes from.

English word in the advertisement	Word from other language
beautiful	*chocolat*
provide	*catour*
explore	*praevius*
perfect	*buffet*
friend	*maintenir*
previous	*explorare*
chocolate	*beau*
cater	*providere*
buffet	*perfectus*
maintain	*freund*

2 Use your dictionary to find out:
- the definition of the English word
- the language the English word comes from.

 Sentence level

Tenses

> The tense of a verb helps us to talk about the time at which an action takes place. When the words 'will' or 'shall' are put in front of a verb this is called the **future tense**.

Example

Look at the use of tense in this sentence:

> Present tense

> Command

*"All rides **are** fully guided, so **no need** to look at the map every two minutes, and with our support vehicle close at hand, all **you'll** need to have with you is your water supply and your favourite chocolate bar – and **we'll** even supply that!"*

> Future tense

> Future tense

1 What do you think are the effects of the writer's use of the future tense and command language in this sentence? Think about the persuasive purpose of the sentence.

Taking part in a discussion

You are going to work in a group of four. A live television programme has asked you to take part in a discussion about what children enjoy on holiday weekends. Spend some time brainstorming ideas on the following topics:

- indoor games – board or computer games
- outdoor activities – challenges, assault courses
- sports
- discos and night-time entertainment
- outings and visits.

When you have completed your brainstorm, divide up the different topics so that each member of the group has a fair share of the information. Make notes on your assigned topic and be prepared to answer questions from the rest of the class who will be the live TV audience. As you watch the other groups perform, think of challenging questions to ask them.

Writing to persuade

You are the customer relations manager of a holiday company called Funtastic Weekends. Your company is running a promotion where two adults can go on holiday for the price of one, and children go for free.

Your job is to write letters to all of your customers encouraging them to take advantage of this offer and come again on a Funtastic Weekend holiday.

You could use some of the ideas from the speaking and listening activity in your writing. You are going to write a formal letter as you don't know your customers that well. This means that your letter needs to be set out correctly. Use the writing frame on page 74 to help you to set out the letter.

Funtastic
Weekends

West Street
Hertford
HT 1DL

Write the name and address of the person you are writing to.

**West Street
Hertford
HT 1DL**

Any Town
Any County
ON1 1AN

Date

Dear _____

I am writing to tell you about a new deal from Funtastic Weekends. First we are offering ...

As you know, kids will love ...

Adults will want to take advantage of ...

A new attraction for the family is ...

Remember, a Funtastic Weekend is a great holiday for all the family because ...

Yours sincerely

Word-processed formal letters use block addresses — commas are not used.

Date usually comes under the address.

Get to the point straightaway — use block paragraphs rather than indenting.

Give other reasons for your customer to come on a Funtastic Weekend.

Remind your customer why a Funtastic Weekend is fun for adults as well as children.

Give details about any new attractions that Funtastic Weekends offer.

Give your customer a final message encouraging them to book another holiday.

Sign the letter.

Print your name and title.

Use this when you know the name of the person you are writing to. If you don't know their name you would end: 'Yours faithfully'.

Leisure

Unit 9: Argue

Writing to argue is closely related to persuasive writing and is a form of discursive writing. You are going to read a newspaper article which takes the form of an argument for and against children playing computer games. In this article, the points made by the author are supported with facts and expert opinions. Once the two sides of the argument are presented, the author puts forward his or her own view.

T Text level: reading

Pre-reading

Do you play computer games? If so, how often? What do you like or dislike about playing computer games?

Exploring different views

1 Make a list of the points the writer uses for and against allowing children to play computer games.

Example

For: Game players are more intelligent and get better jobs.

Against:

> When writers want to make their arguments stronger, they support their points with **evidence.** In the article on the opposite page, the writer quotes some experts to support his or her own viewpoints. For instance, Simon Fullarton is a computer expert who gives examples of games that build problem-solving skills.

2 What other experts are quoted and what do they say? Why do you think their opinions are important?

3 Why do you think the writer uses the term 'geek' to describe Fullarton? Why does he use speech marks here?

4 What other ways does the writer support the points in his or her article?

5 Not all articles like this end with a conclusion, but this one does. What is it?

6 Which of the arguments do you agree with and why? Before you write anything, discuss your ideas with a partner.

Computer games: learning aid or brain drain?

A new research review published by the Home Office suggests that children who play computer games may actually be more intelligent than average and are more likely to go on to university and higher ranking jobs.

Simon Fullarton, a self-professed computer 'geek', supports this view. 'Games don't just give you a buzz – they require intelligence and intuition,' says Fullarton. 'Take a game like Half Life, in which you're a character in a world that's been taken over by zombies that are after you. To escape you have to deal with natural disasters, pick up visual clues, avoid capture and devise strategies. It's all about problem solving.'

Moreover, Fullarton is a prime example of a high-achieving computer geek. Fullarton is now a Cisco computer networking engineer. In this highly demanding job he can earn around £1,000 a day.

Many experts believe that the popularity of computer games amongst children will continue to grow, as computer skills are now essential in the modern world and these games help to develop them. 'My eldest son is dyslexic and the skills he has built up through games have helped enormously,' says Martina Milburn, head of the charity Children in Need. 'For example, he was able to do his GCSE revision using a CD-ROM.'

However, Milburn does sound a warning note: 'I don't let my boys play the more violent games.'

In the past two decades, several research studies have suggested that computer games cause aggression amongst children. In fact, one study showed that 40 out of the 47 most popular games had violence as a major theme.

In addition, some of the Home Office research suggests that children who play computer games can become withdrawn and begin to lose a sense of their own worth. They develop addictive personalities and lose their grip on reality. All of this, it says, could lead to youngsters getting into trouble with the law.

Dr Mark Griffiths, an expert on the effects of video games, says that while more research is needed it now seems clear that a child's play after watching a violent video game becomes more aggressive and anti-social.

On the other hand, some experts have suggested that playing aggressive video games has a relaxing effect by channelling and releasing aggression. This is a view shared by nearly all game players, not to mention the New York Police Department, who told the makers of the infamous joyriding game Grand Theft Auto: 'We'd rather they did it in your game than on the street.'

The Home Office report reached no specific conclusions about the wider fears that parents may have about violence in games because the research continues to be contradictory. But the finding that children who play games are more intelligent than average and more likely to go into higher education must be some comfort.

Dictionary check

intuition intelligent guessing
addictive personality the type of person who can't stop doing something
anti-social unwilling to mix with other people
infamous having a bad reputation
specific particular
contradictory disagreeing with itself

 Word level

Link words and phrases

> Writers often use words and phrases like 'however', 'but', 'on the other hand' and 'moreover' to link ideas in their writing. These **link words** are usually at the beginnings of sentences, and they help the reader to make a connection between ideas in one sentence with those in another.

1 Find these link words in the newspaper article. Which ideas do they connect?

> moreover   however
> on the other hand   but

2 Below there are four pairs of sentences. Which link words can be used to connect each of the pairs? It may be possible to use more than one link word for each example. The first one is done for you.

a) ▶ Short bursts of computer gaming may actually boost reflexes.
    ▶ Over time extensive and repetitive use can cause repetitive strain injuries.

Example

Short bursts of computer gaming may actually boost reflexes. However, over time extensive and repetitive use can cause repetitive strain injuries.

b) ▶ I don't like violent computer games.
    ▶ I don't think they do any harm.

c) ▶ Some research suggests that children become more violent after playing computer games.
    ▶ Other research suggests that violence cannot be connected to computer games.

d) ▶ It's clear that computer games are bad for health and social development.
    ▶ Evidence also suggests that they may be helping to create a violent society.

Using quotations

One way in which writers provide evidence for an argument is to quote an expert. **Speech marks** are used to show which words the expert used. These are also called **quotation marks**. In the article, speech marks are used to show the reader what Simon Fullarton is saying. Look at how this example is punctuated.

open speech mark

'Games don't just give you a buzz – they require intelligence and intuition,' says Fullarton.

comma before closing speech mark

full stop at the end of the sentence

1 Rewrite this extract from an argument about computer gaming. Put in the correct speech punctuation.

Since the early 1990s we have been concerned that children do not socialise enough or do enough physical exercise said Dr Clapham. Moreover she continued there is a lot of evidence that poor fitness in youth can seriously affect health later in life

2 Write a paragraph about the dangers of computer gaming. Use the link words and quote the experts.

Hunching over a computer causes terrible posture in children.

Chris Brooks, GP

I've stopped seeing my friends so much since I got a Playstation.

Mike Smith, 14

My son Mike doesn't do his homework properly now he has a Playstation.

Jane Smith, Mother

Presenting an argument

Work in two sets of pairs. One pair will argue that computer games are bad for you, and one pair will argue that computer games are not bad for you.

▶ First, work with your partner to plan all the arguments in favour of your ideas about computer games – think of good reasons to back up your views.

▶ Then test out these arguments on the pair of pupils who are arguing the opposite view.

▶ Their task is then to give arguments against your arguments!

▶ Practise your arguing for and against each other's arguments until you are ready to present your debate to the rest of the class.

▶ Be prepared to answer further questions from the class about your ideas.

▶ At the end, the class can vote on which pair of pupils argued the most convincingly.

The planning frame on the opposite page will help you.

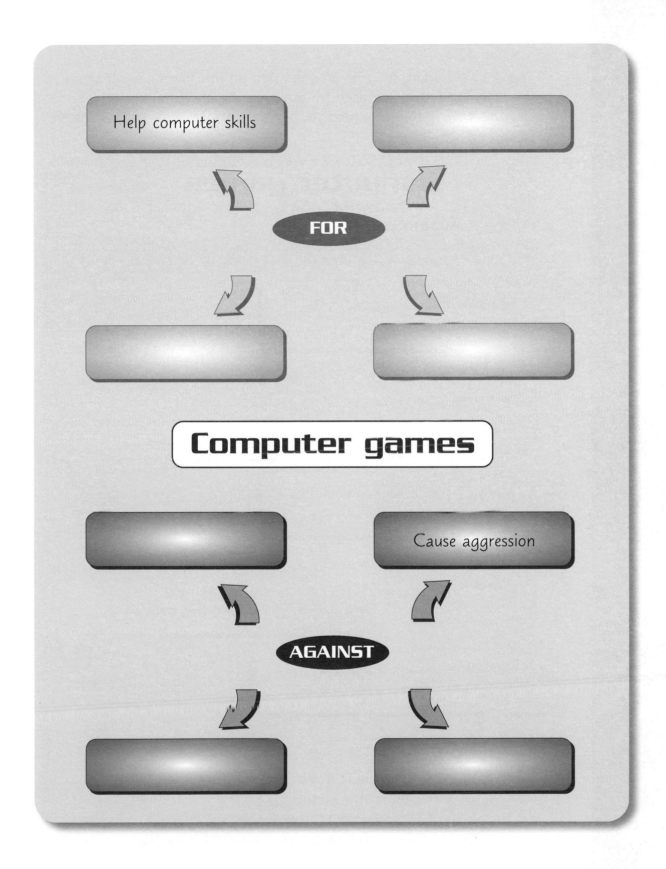

Help computer skills

FOR

Computer games

Cause aggression

AGAINST

Writing to argue

You are now going to write an argument on this theme. Look again at the planning frame you used for the speaking and listening activity. Use this writing frame to help you with the structure of the argument.

Computer games

Against   **For**

- Some people think that a good reason not to play computer games is ...
- They think this because ...

- However, many pupils believe that ...
- Their reasoning is ...
- A second point in favour is ...
- They believe this because ...

- On the other hand, some people say ...
- This is because ...

- A third argument in favour of playing computer games is ...
- They believe this because ...

- Against this, though, some think that ...

- To conclude, I would argue that ...
- I think this because ...

Leisure

Advisory writing sets out to guide and be helpful to the reader. It is often seen in magazines, leaflets and newspapers. The problem page in a magazine is a good example of writing that attempts to give the reader advice. Sometimes, however, advice can be found in works of literature, such as the famous poem 'If ...' by Rudyard Kipling.

Pre-reading

Where do you get advice? Do you always follow the advice you are given?

Identifying the main points

1 In the first line of the poem, Kipling advises us to keep calm when everyone around us panics. Working in a group of four, take a verse each and, in your own words, write down what the reader should and should not do by looking at the advice your verse gives. Use a grid like the one below to record this information and then compare what you have written with the rest of your group.

What we should do	What we should not do

2 What do you think of Kipling's advice? Choose one piece of his advice and write about a time when this advice might have been good for you or for someone you know well.

If ...

If you can keep your head when all about you
Are losing theirs and blaming it on you,
If you can trust yourself when all men doubt you,
But make allowance for their doubting too;
If you can wait and not be tired by waiting,
Or being lied about, don't deal in lies,
Or being hated, don't give way to hating,
And yet don't look too good, nor talk too wise:

If you can dream – and not make dreams your master;
If you can think – and not make thoughts your aim;
If you can meet with Triumph and Disaster
And treat those two impostors just the same;
If you can bear to hear the truth you've spoken
Twisted by knaves to make a trap for fools,
Or watch the things you gave your life to, broken,
And stoop and build 'em up with worn-out tools:

If you can make one heap of all your winnings
And risk it on one turn of pitch-and-toss,
And lose, and start again at your beginnings
And never breathe a word about your loss;
If you can force your heart and nerve and sinew
To serve your turn long after they are gone,
And so hold on when there is nothing in you
Except the Will which says to them: 'Hold on!'

If you can talk with crowds and keep your virtue,
Or walk with Kings – nor lose the common touch,
If neither foes nor loving friends can hurt you,
If all men count with you, but none too much;
If you can fill the unforgiving minute
With sixty seconds' worth of distance run,
Yours is the Earth and everything that's in it,
And – which is more – you'll be a Man, my son!

Rudyard Kipling

Dictionary check

impostors people who pretend to be someone else
knaves dishonest people
pitch and toss an old fashioned game where coins are thrown at a marker
sinew muscle

 **W** Word level

Rhyme and apostrophes

Words that sound alike are said to **rhyme**. You often find rhymes when lines of poetry sound the same at the end.

> Example
>
> *If you can wait and not be tired by waiting,*
> *Or being lied about, don't deal in lies,*
> *Or being hated, don't give way to hating,*
> *And yet don't look too good, nor talk too wise:*

Even though 'lies' and 'wise' are spelt differently they still sound alike.

1 Look carefully at the line endings in Kipling's poem. Pick out the pairs of words that rhyme.

2 Select a pair of rhyming words that are spelt differently. Brainstorm as many words as you can that also fit this rhyme. Use a dictionary to check your spelling.

An **apostrophe** looks like a comma hanging in the air and is used in two ways:

- to show that a letter has been left out – 'I am' becomes 'I'm'

- to show possession or belonging – 'the homework belonging to Jamie' can become 'Jamie's homework'.

3 In the poem there are several examples where the apostrophe has been used to show that a letter has been left out. Copy out and complete the grid on the opposite page by picking out these examples and writing down how the word would appear if the apostrophe was not used.

With apostrophe	Without apostrophe
don't	
you've	
'em	
that's	
you'll	

4 There is only one example of the use of the apostrophe in the poem to show possession. Find it and copy it out.

S Sentence level

Using punctuation to clarify meaning

The poem contains many different types of punctuation, but doesn't include any full stops.

1 Look again at the poem and pick out the different types of punctuation that are used.

2 How many sentences can you count in the poem? Does this surprise you?

3 Choose one verse of the poem and, with a partner, practise reading it out, but ignore all of the punctuation. Then read it out again, making sure that you pause in the right places. Give an example of a part of the poem where the punctuation helps you to understand the meaning.

4 Copy out the following sentences and put in the correct punctuation to help make the meaning clear.

   a) You should eat fresh fruit muesli yoghurt and wholemeal bread for a healthy diet
   b) The best way to keep fit is by walking jogging or running cycling swimming or rowing and playing sports such as football hockey and rugby
   c) I want to let you know what I think about football soccers the most exciting sport there is

SL Speaking and listening

Advice phone-in

A daytime television show has organised an advice phone-in for young people with problems at school. In pairs, carry out your own phone-in, working in this way:

- one person plays the part of the caller
- one person plays the part of the person giving advice.

Here are some of the subjects on which people have rung in to ask for advice:

 **Phone-in**

Something getting you down? Don't worry, agony uncle Andy is here to help …

Someone in my class at school has been telling lies about me to other people. I think my closest friend has been listening to these lies and has stopped talking to me.

Everyone in my class at school calls me 'boffin'. When we do a test, and I get good marks, I always have to keep quiet about it for fear of being laughed at.

I really like somebody in my class, but I can't seem to build up the courage to talk to them. How can I get them to notice me?

Please help! I can't seem to concentrate on anything at school. My teachers all say I am a dreamer and never pay attention in class. What can I do?

With your partner rehearse the telephone conversation between the caller and the person giving the advice. Make sure that you give good advice and try to make your conversation believable. When you have finished practising your performance, show it to the rest of the class.

Writing to advise

You are now going to write an informal letter setting out your advice in more detail to one of the callers.

Use the planning frame below to help you to organise your ideas.

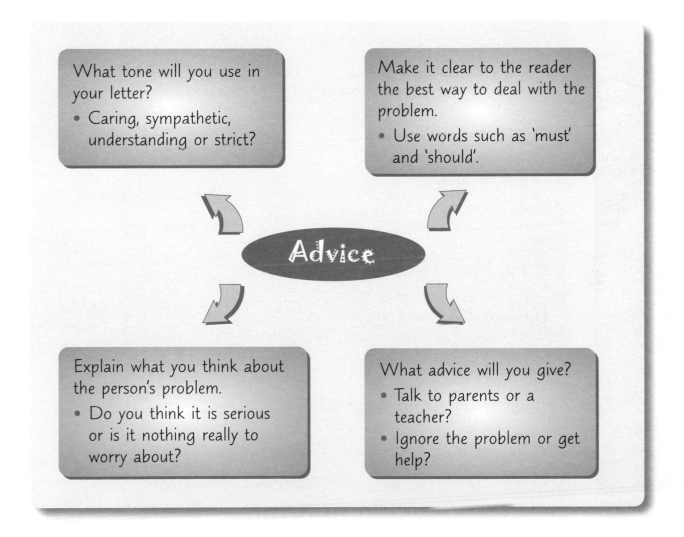

What tone will you use in your letter?
• Caring, sympathetic, understanding or strict?

Make it clear to the reader the best way to deal with the problem.
• Use words such as 'must' and 'should'.

Advice

Explain what you think about the person's problem.
• Do you think it is serious or is it nothing really to worry about?

What advice will you give?
• Talk to parents or a teacher?
• Ignore the problem or get help?

Use this writing frame to help you to structure your letter. Remember this is an informal letter to somebody that you have already spoken to, so keep your letter friendly and relaxed.

Your address

Date

Dear _____

I am writing to give you some more advice about ...

You must not worry about ...

This is because ...

I think you should ...

You really need to ...

This is would be a good idea as ...

My final advice to you is ...

If you need any further advice you should ...

Yours,

Use the first name of the person you are writing to and remember to put a comma after it.

Explain why you are writing.

Set out your guidance and advice about the problem.

Write your first name here.

Reading log ▶▶▶

In this section you have looked at texts that:

- ▶ try to persuade the reader
- ▶ argue the case for and against a subject
- ▶ offer the reader advice.

You will come across texts like these in a lot of the reading that you do in your everyday life.

▶ For a week, keep a reading log to keep track of the different texts you see that try to persuade, argue or advise. Make a note of what the texts are trying to do and how effective you think that they are.

Texts that persuade
A flyer advertising a school disco

Effectiveness
The flyer mentioned the types of music that will be played, which included groups that I like. It also showed a picture of the DJ who will be performing.

Texts that argue

Effectiveness

Texts that advise

Effectiveness

Snakes and ladders ▶▶▶

With a partner, play the snakes and ladders game. If you are not sure if an answer is correct, write it down and check it with your teacher.
Once you have completed the game, work with your partner to create your own snakes and ladders game by brainstorming questions about the topics that you have learned about in this section.

Finish

29 Go back eight spaces.

28 Go back five spaces.

27 Go to finish.

26 Complete this linking word: 'more ____'.

21 Complete this linking word: 'never___less'.

22 Where should the apostrophe go in this sentence: 'James books were untidy.'?

23 You have ten seconds to correct this spelling: 'truimph'.

24 Go on two spaces.

25 'Freund' is like the English word...

20 Name one way that writers make their arguments stronger.

19 Miss a turn.

18 Go on five spaces.

17 You have thirty seconds to list ten words that rhyme with 'falling'.

16 Complete the phrase 'on the _____ hand'.

11 What letter has been left out in 'I'm'.

12 Go on eight spaces.

13 You have thirty seconds to list ten words that rhyme with 'fun'.

14 Speech marks are also known as...

15 Go back eight spaces.

10 Go back to start.

9 You have thirty seconds to correct these spellings: commputer viollence agresivve.

8 Miss a turn.

7 The word 'chocolate' comes from which language?

6 List six linking words.

Start

2 Persuasive language is usually positive language. True or false?

3 You have one minute to name four places where you would see persuasive language.

4 Move on two spaces.

5 You have fifteen seconds to correct the spelling of: acomoddation.

Science

Unit 11: Analyse

Analytical writing is a very careful examination of what something is or why something has happened. You are going to read an article that analyses a new scientific treatment that could dramatically increase the size of people's muscles and help them to recover more quickly from injury. The writer also examines the controversy that this new treatment is causing among people involved in sport.

Pre-reading

What do you think about athletes taking drugs to improve their performances? Do you think that we should use new scientific techniques to improve our health and fitness?

Balancing different views

1 What makes the 'supermouse' different from other mice? Explain how the IGF-1 protein works.

2 The article attempts to analyse some of the positive and negative effects of drugs such as IGF-1 protein. Copy out and complete the table below by listing the advantages and disadvantages of these drugs.

Advantages	Disadvantages
repairs muscles	could help athletes to cheat in sports events

3 The article includes opinions from different people about the use of IGF-1 protein. Some of these people see the good side of the treatment, whilst others look at the bad side. List the different people who comment and explain whether they are in favour of the treatment or against it. In some cases you will need to look carefully at what they say and do.

From supermouse to **superman ...**

American scientists at the University of Pennsylvania have made a scientific breakthrough that could change the face of sport. Researchers have created a genetically modified supermouse with indestructible muscles three times the size of those of a normal mouse. This powerful rodent can even climb a ladder whilst carrying three times its own body weight with ease.

The principle behind the experiment was a simple one. The research team, led by Dr H. Lee Sweeney, injected a new-born mouse with a synthetic gene that encouraged its muscle cells to create more IGF-1 (insulin-like growth factor -1) protein. This protein stimulates muscle growth and also repairs muscles when they have been damaged. In young people IGF-1 is produced during exercise and helps develop bigger muscles. However as we get older, the body's production of IGF-1 slows down. This means that our muscles start to deteriorate and we become slower and weaker.

Age, however, has not slowed the supermouse. The synthetic gene that he was injected with produced huge muscles that have kept on producing IGF-1 protein. Even as it approaches mouse old age its muscles and strength remain at their youthful levels. 'The muscles maintain their size through the whole life of the animal,' reports Dr Sweeney.

This scientific advance does bring with it problems, especially for those in charge of competitive sport. 'If this is being done on mice, humans aren't far behind,' comments Bengt Saltin, a member of the World Anti-Doping Agency (WADA). The prospect of genetically modified athletes implanted with the IGF -1 gene dominating at future Olympics and World Championships horrifies the sports authorities. WADA, which was founded by the International Olympic Committee (IOC), takes the threat of genetic manipulation in sport so seriously that it is hosting an international conference on the subject.

In the past, cheats who sought to improve their performances through the use of banned steroids and supplements knew that they ran the risk of being caught by drug tests. In the future athletes with genetic implants will be much harder to catch, as Gary Wadler, a professor at the New York University School of Medicine explains: 'The only way you'll be able to prove an athlete is cheating is through a muscle biopsy, and that's not going to happen.'

The outlook for sport in the brave new world of genetic research and manipulation is not all bad. 'We have to accept that some of these enhancements will be wonderful, especially for athletes who are injured,' admits Harri Syvasalmi, WADA's secretary general. A report published by researchers from the University of Pittsburgh shows that recovery from sports-related injuries can be speeded up and improved through the introduction of genes, like the IGF-1 gene, that stimulate muscle growth. 'One day injured tendons, cartilage or ligaments will be repaired through an injection,' says Gary Wadler. This could save health services millions of pounds in patient care and therapy, as well as shortening the painful recovery period for the patient.

The question of whether genetic manipulation should be stopped remains. We may shiver at the thought of genetic experimentation creating a football team with eleven David Beckhams (unless you're a Manchester United fan), but the idea of heading into old age with the body of a fit and healthy twenty-year-old is an appealing one. If science can help us to combat the damage caused by ageing, why shouldn't we use it?

Dictionary check

genetically modified changing an animal's genes with a special treatment
manipulation careful changing
biopsy removal of tissue or fluid from a living body
enhancements improvements

Working out the meaning of words

Acronyms are words that are made up from the first letters of other words, such as DJ which is short for 'disc jockey' and BBC which stands for 'British Broadcasting Corporation'. Using acronyms saves time for the writer and the reader.

1 Pick out any acronyms that you can find in the article and explain what they stand for.

Often, we can work out the meaning of difficult words by looking at the words around them in the sentence.

American scientists at the University of Pennsylvania have made a scientific breakthrough that could change the face of sport.

In the first sentence we learn that scientists have made a 'breakthrough'. The reader may not be too sure what 'breakthrough' means, but because the word 'change' follows shortly afterwards, we can probably guess that the word has something to do with a change. When we check the dictionary definition of the word 'breakthrough' we find out that it means 'a major leap forward in knowledge'.

2 In each of the following sentences work out the meaning of the highlighted word by looking at other words in the same sentence for clues. Pick out the word that provides the clue and then give the dictionary definition of the word in bold.

a) This protein stimulates muscle growth and also **repairs** muscles when they have been damaged.

b) This means that our muscles start to **deteriorate** and we become slower and slower.

c) This could save health services millions of pounds in patient care and **therapy**, as well as shortening the painful recovery period for the patient.

Topic sentences in paragraphs

Topic sentences are sentences that make it clear to the reader what the paragraph is about. They make it much easier for a reader to follow the meaning of a text by acting like signposts in a paragraph.

Topic sentence

The outlook for sport in the brave new world of genetic research and manipulation is not all bad. 'We have to accept that some of these enhancements will be wonderful, especially for athletes who are injured,' admits Harri Syvasalmi, WADA's secretary general. A report published by researchers from the University of Pittsburgh shows that recovery from sports-related injuries can be speeded up and improved through the introduction of genes, like the IGF-1 gene, that stimulate muscle growth.

Details that show the positive effects of genetic research

1 Pick out the topic sentences from the first three paragraphs of the article.

2 Look at the following topic sentences and explain what you would expect each paragraph to be about.

   a) This scientific advance does bring with it problems, especially for those in charge of competitive sport.

   b) In the past, cheats who sought to improve their performances through the use of banned steroids and supplements knew that they ran the risk of being caught by drug tests.

   c) The question of whether genetic manipulation should be stopped remains.

3 Look at the paragraphs in the article that the topic sentences in question 2 are taken from. Discuss with a partner whether you think your answers to question 2 are correct.

Discussing a situation

You are going to act out a role-play on the following subject:

> Sam is a keen sportsperson and a member of several school teams, playing sport several evenings a week after school and also practising at lunch times. Recently, Sam has been late in handing in homework and some people have started to worry about the amount of time Sam spends playing sports.

Here are some comments.

> I've always liked playing sport. I think that it helps to develop different skills and I don't let it interfere with my class work.
>
> *Sam*

> Sam has never missed a homework deadline before. Sometimes, when sports practice finishes, Sam comes home really tired.
>
> *Sam's Mum*

> Sam never lets the team down. I personally think that it is healthy to exercise the body and not just the mind.
>
> *Sam's PE teacher*

> Sam is a sensible pupil, but it is important to keep a balance between school work and sporting activities.
>
> *Sam's form teacher*

Work in a group of four. Each pupil should play a different character and think about the opinions this person would have about the situation. The school has set up a meeting to discuss Sam's situation. Think about the questions your character would want to ask the others. Act out a scene where all the characters discuss whether Sam should spend less time playing sport, making sure that each member of the group gets the chance to ask and answer a question.

Writing to analyse

For this writing task, you are going to write a piece of analysis by answering the question 'What makes a good student?' To do this you need to make notes about the qualities that a good student possesses. You should also give examples of times when these qualities are important and include different people's opinions. Use the planning frame to help you.

Use the following writing frame to help you write your analysis. Remember to use topic sentences to help the reader to understand what each paragraph is about.

Introduction

In this essay I am writing to analyse what makes a good student. There are, in my opinion, four main qualities that a good student possesses. These are ...

First paragraph

First ...
The reasons this quality is so important is because ...

Second paragraph

The second quality a good student possesses is ...
This is vital because ...

Third paragraph

Another important quality is ...
I think this is useful because ...

Fourth paragraph

Lastly ...
A good student needs to be this because ...

Conclusion

To conclude, there are four qualities that a good student has. These are ...
If I had to pick one of these four qualities as the main one I would say that ...

Science   Unit 12: Review

Writers of reviews look back at something they have read or seen and try to help the reader to decide whether it is worth seeing or buying. There are reviews of books, films and TV programmes, as well as music CDs and computer games. You are going to read a review of *Jurassic Park*, a 1993 film about a scientist who brings dinosaurs back to life.

T Text level: reading

Pre-reading

What would you want to find out from a review of a film?

Inferring meanings

1 What role does the actor Richard Attenborough play in the film?

2 How is the character of the mathematician described? Use a dictionary to find out what this means.

> Writers do not always make obvious what they think about a subject. They will often **imply** or suggest their meaning by using carefully chosen words or phrases. As readers, we **infer** or 'read between the lines' and by thinking what the words used suggest, we work out what is meant.

3 The highlighted words in the following sentences hint at the writer's thoughts. Can you work out the implied meaning? The first one is done for you.

Example

    a) *The plot is as **tiny as the preserved insect** from which DNA is extracted.*
    Implied meaning – the plot of the film is simple and unimportant.

    b) Dinosaur experts Sam Neill and Laura Dern along with the wise-cracking mathematician Jeff Goldblum, kids Tim and Lex, and lawyer Martin Ferrero all **jump onboard for the inevitable terror trip**.

    c) The director **cranks up** the tension.

    d) But this is a **roller-coaster ride of a movie** and one that I'd definitely see again.

Jurassic Park

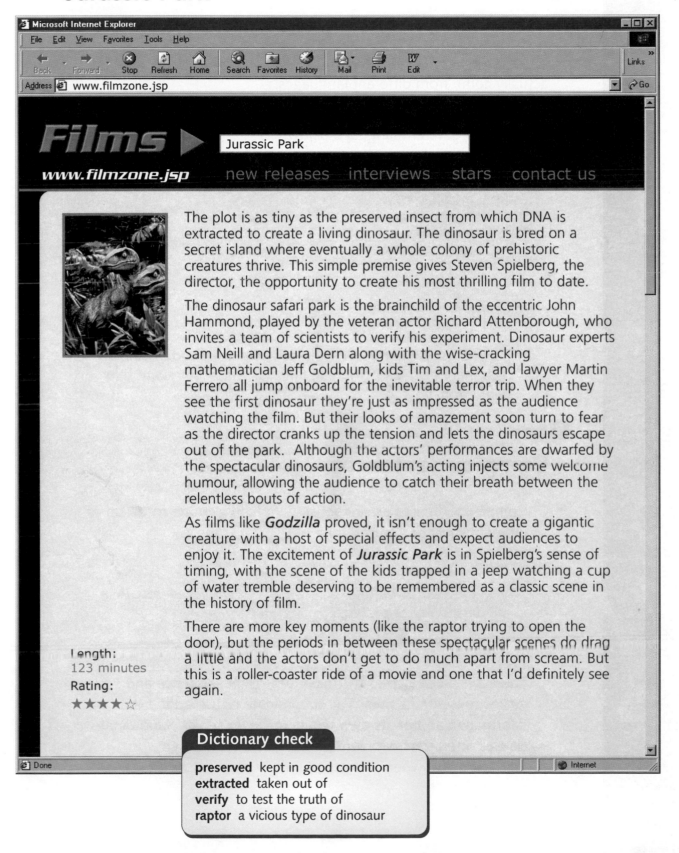

Microsoft Internet Explorer

File   Edit   View   Favorites   Tools   Help

Back   Forward   Stop   Refresh   Home   Search   Favorites   History   Mail   Print   Edit   Links

Address www.filmzone.jsp   Go

Films ▶ Jurassic Park

www.filmzone.jsp   new releases   interviews   stars   contact us

The plot is as tiny as the preserved insect from which DNA is extracted to create a living dinosaur. The dinosaur is bred on a secret island where eventually a whole colony of prehistoric creatures thrive. This simple premise gives Steven Spielberg, the director, the opportunity to create his most thrilling film to date.

The dinosaur safari park is the brainchild of the eccentric John Hammond, played by the veteran actor Richard Attenborough, who invites a team of scientists to verify his experiment. Dinosaur experts Sam Neill and Laura Dern along with the wise-cracking mathematician Jeff Goldblum, kids Tim and Lex, and lawyer Martin Ferrero all jump onboard for the inevitable terror trip. When they see the first dinosaur they're just as impressed as the audience watching the film. But their looks of amazement soon turn to fear as the director cranks up the tension and lets the dinosaurs escape out of the park. Although the actors' performances are dwarfed by the spectacular dinosaurs, Goldblum's acting injects some welcome humour, allowing the audience to catch their breath between the relentless bouts of action.

As films like **Godzilla** proved, it isn't enough to create a gigantic creature with a host of special effects and expect audiences to enjoy it. The excitement of **Jurassic Park** is in Spielberg's sense of timing, with the scene of the kids trapped in a jeep watching a cup of water tremble deserving to be remembered as a classic scene in the history of film.

There are more key moments (like the raptor trying to open the door), but the periods in between these spectacular scenes do drag a little and the actors don't get to do much apart from scream. But this is a roller-coaster ride of a movie and one that I'd definitely see again.

Length:
123 minutes
Rating:
★★★★☆

Dictionary check

preserved kept in good condition
extracted taken out of
verify to test the truth of
raptor a vicious type of dinosaur

Done   Internet

 W Word level

Vocabulary

There are several words used in the passage on page 103 that actually come from different languages.

a) Find the words in the passage that match up with the words from a different language below:

Word from a different language	Word in passage
verus	
terrere	
tensus	
enjoier	
momemtum	

b) Now look up the meaning of each of these words in the dictionary and see if you can find out which language they come from.

S Sentence level

Complex sentences

Complex sentences are longer sentences, which are made up of different parts or 'clauses'.

Main clause

Example

The dinosaur is bred on a secret island where eventually a whole colony of prehistoric creatures thrive.

Subordinate clause

The main clause carries the main idea of the sentence and makes sense on its own. The subordinate clause adds extra information and on its own would make no sense. Subordinate clauses often start with words like 'where', 'although', 'because', 'if' ,'when', 'which', 'until', 'unless'.

1 Identify the main clause and the subordinate clause in the following sentences:

    a) I decided to go to the cinema after going shopping because the new Harry Potter film was showing.

    b) She believed that she had seen the video at the cinema last year, although she wasn't sure.

    c) Unless you are extremely brave, you should not go to see horror films.

    d) When you go to see *Jurassic Park*, you will thoroughly enjoy it.

2 Use the following clauses to make **four** different complex sentences, each made up of a main clause and a subordinate clause:

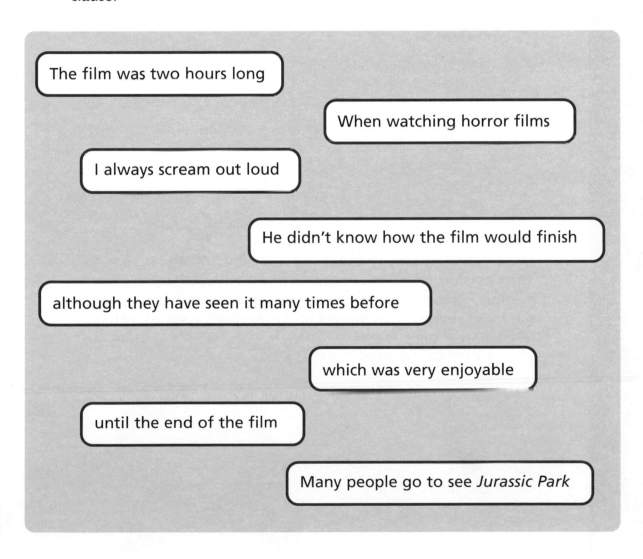

The film was two hours long

When watching horror films

I always scream out loud

He didn't know how the film would finish

although they have seen it many times before

which was very enjoyable

until the end of the film

Many people go to see *Jurassic Park*

Contributing to a discussion

You have been asked to appear on a Saturday morning children's television programme to take part in the section of the show where new books, films and TV programmes are reviewed. Work in a group of four with:

- one of you playing the presenter of the programme
- the other three of you reviewing a film, book or TV programme.

The presenter should	The reviewers should
▶ give an introduction to the film, book or TV programme ▶ think of six interesting questions to ask the reviewers ▶ sum up the reviewers' opinions about what they have seen or read.	▶ explain what the story is about ▶ say what they think about the actors or characters in the film, book or TV programme ▶ describe their favourite scene or passage ▶ be prepared to answer the presenter's questions.

Make notes to help you and rehearse what you are going to say. Think carefully about your opinions and listen to what the other members of the review team have to say. When you are ready, you can show your work to the rest of the class, who will act as the live television audience.

Writing a review

You are going to write a review of a film, book or TV programme. Use the notes you made for the speaking and listening activity to help you. Try to help the reader decide whether the film, book or TV programme is worth seeing or buying and remember to give reasons to support your opinions.

The planning frame on page 108 may help you with the task.

▶ Tell the reader what you are going to review.
■ The name of the book/film/TV programme I am reviewing is ...

▶ Give some information about who starred in/wrote/directed it.
■ It is the new book/film/TV programme from ...

▶ Explain who is it aimed at — young children, teenagers or the whole family?
■ The target audience for this book/film/TV programme is ...

▶ Tell the reader a little about the story — how it begins and the way the plot develops, but remember not to give away the ending!
■ The story is about ...

▶ Give your opinions about the actors or characters — good or bad? Believable or unrealistic?
■ I think that the actors/characters are ...

▶ Tell the reader about your favourite part and explain why you liked it.
■ The best part of the book/film/TV programme is where ...
■ I liked this scene because ...

▶ Sum up in a few words what you thought of it overall — would you recommend it or do you think people should avoid it?
■ To conclude, I think this book/film/TV programme rates ...

Help box

Try to use complex sentences where possible.
The following words may be useful:

where   when   before   though
   unless   if   because   which
until   although   after   so   during

Science   Unit 13: Comment

Comments may be read in a variety of places, from newspapers and magazines to websites. By their nature they are generally informal in tone – the written version of something that might be said. You are going to read some comments for an online debate about the subject of human cloning. The topic of cloning has gone from being a matter of science fiction in films such as *Jurassic Park*, to becoming scientific fact when researchers cloned a sheep.

Pre-reading

Do you think human beings should be cloned? Would you want to be cloned?

Exploring different views

1 Sum up the views of each of the three people who are making comments in the online debate about cloning.

2 What facts do you learn about cloning from this online debate?

3 Do you think this debate succeeds in getting the reader more interested in the cloning controversy? What is your opinion about cloning?

Microsoft Internet Explorer

File   Edit   View   Favorites   Tools   Help

Back · Forward · Stop   Refresh   Home   Search   Favorites   History   Mail   Print   Edit   Links »

Address http://talk.guardian.co.uk   Go

GuardianUnlimited
The**talk**

Guardian Talk

Online debate

Home

Uk latest

Talk

Search

Help

Live debate, Thursday 9 August, 4pm

Should humans be cloned?

Do you think human beings should be cloned? Guardian science editor Tim Radford will be live online at 4pm, Thursday 9 August to debate the issue with geneticist Dr Robin Lovell-Badge, head of the division of developmental genetics at the GMRC National Institute for Medicine.

M.Rice

I'd be interested to know what you think the benefits of human cloning would actually be in the long run. I can see the medical benefits of stem cell research, and growing limbs or brain tissue, but I fail to see the point of making a copy of myself.

It doesn't increase my lifespan in any way, because the clone isn't actually me. It could develop entirely differently to the way I did and become a completely different person. This doesn't seem to help keep anyone else alive, either.

The idea of cloning as an aid to infertile couples seems absolutely bizarre. I can't have a child, but I can have a mini-me? Yuk! Besides, infertile couples have a wide and growing range of options for having children already.

So, I don't see the point at all. From a philosophical point of view, I suppose I don't think anyone should be stopped from cloning unless the act of doing so is going to hurt or harm the clone. But I kind of wish the scientists didn't feel the need to do this.

T.Radford - Reply

I wouldn't want a clone of me either. But the thing is, it wouldn't be me: it would be someone with exactly my genetic potential whose ideas, attitudes, physique and intellect had been shaped by the world he grew up in. He'd probably be my height, look pretty much like me, go bald in the middle of his head at about the same time and need glasses. But he'd be very different. Still doesn't make cloning a great idea.

Dr Lovell-Badge - Reply

Just an added point – there are very few scientists who want to clone humans. There are many good reasons for doing so with animals, but essentially none with humans. The few individuals or groups advocating cloning almost certainly have their own agenda. This may be the Raelians, who perhaps mean well, but are misguided, or Dr Severino and colleagues, who want to play God and get fame and fortune – at the expense of infertile couples.

Done   Internet

Dictionary check

stem cell research special cells from a newly fertilised human egg programmed to grow in any part of the body, ear, heart, etc. Doctors can replace the damaged part of the body with new cells
infertile couples people who are unable to conceive children
raelians members of a religious cult

Informal language

Many popular websites use informal or colloquial language to explain ideas and express opinions. Informal language sounds casual and natural and is often very close to spoken language.

Example

I can't have a child, but I can have a mini-me? Yuk!

The colloquial words are 'mini-me' and 'Yuk'. The use of 'can't' instead of 'cannot' also adds to the informal style. Informal language is increasingly seen in e-mails.

1 Pick out other examples of informal language from the online debate.

2 Look at the following sentences and try to match each one to its source.

---

a) What a wicked goal!

b) A fine goal was scored by the centre-forward.

c) Gimme that here now!

d) Hand that over immediately.

e) Text us later if you're coming over.

f) Send a written reply to confirm your attendance.

---

i) A teacher talking to a pupil.

ii) A boy arranging a night out with a friend.

iii) A pupil arguing with a classmate.

iv) An online newspaper report about a football match.

v) An invitation to a dinner-party.

vi) A football fan's e-mail to his friend.

S Sentence level

Expanding sentences

The word 'but' is usually used to link two contrasting ideas in a sentence together. This type of linking word is called a **conjunction**. In the online debate some conjunctions appear at the start of sentences. This is a signal that the writer is using an informal style. Other conjunctions include 'and', 'or', 'if', 'while', 'when', 'where', 'although', 'since', 'because', 'before', 'after' and 'so'.

Example

But I kind of wish the scientists didn't feel the need to do this.

1 Pick out any other examples of conjunctions being used at the start of sentences from the online debate.

2 Copy out and complete the following text by adding conjunctions.

_____ I could clone myself I would_____ I wouldn't want to clone my younger brother. _____ I first heard about cloning I thought it was a scary idea _____ so many people seemed to be against it. _____ I heard doctors talking about the way that cloning could help to cure diseases I changed my mind _____ the possible benefits seemed to outweigh the problems. ____, now I think that cloning is a good idea.

SL Speaking and listening

Role-play and evaluation

You are going to take part in a radio or television phone-in programme about the subject of cloning. Work in a group of four with each member speaking one of the following parts:

- one of you will play the presenter
- one or two will play the expert(s) on cloning
- one or two will play the callers.

Rehearse a three-minute role-play where different callers call the expert(s), asking questions and giving their opinions about cloning. Use the online debate to find out information about cloning.

You will then present your role-play to the rest of the class. When each group has presented its work, make brief notes about:

- how clearly each group spoke
- how interesting their ideas were
- how well they seemed to work together as a group
- how they could improve their overall performance.

Writing to comment

The debate about cloning has continued on a popular website's talk-board. You are going to e-mail a range of comments on the subject of cloning to this talk-board. Try to include a few comments that contain different views from those of your own. The language you are going to use should:

- be brief and to the point
- use informal words
- show your opinion on the subject.

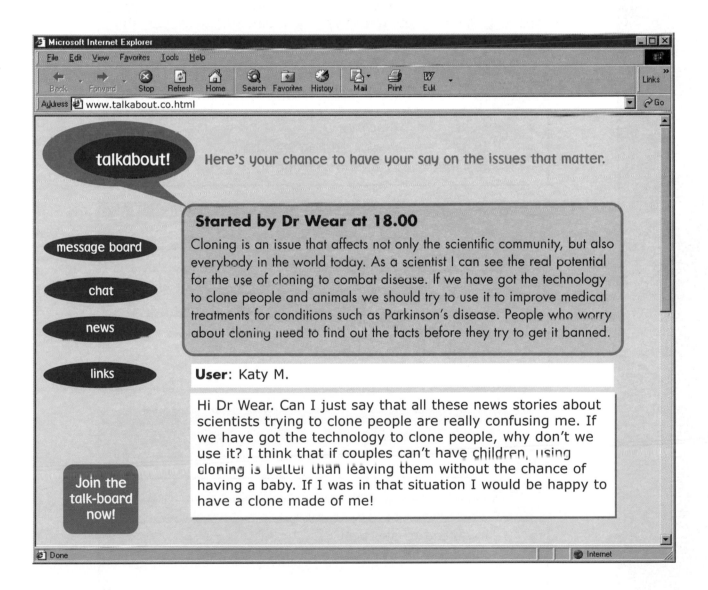

talkabout! Here's your chance to have your say on the issues that matter.

message board

chat

news

links

Join the talk-board now!

Started by Dr Wear at 18.00

Cloning is an issue that affects not only the scientific community, but also everybody in the world today. As a scientist I can see the real potential for the use of cloning to combat disease. If we have got the technology to clone people and animals we should try to use it to improve medical treatments for conditions such as Parkinson's disease. People who worry about cloning need to find out the facts before they try to get it banned.

User: Katy M.

Hi Dr Wear. Can I just say that all these news stories about scientists trying to clone people are really confusing me. If we have got the technology to clone people, why don't we use it? I think that if couples can't have children, using cloning is better than leaving them without the chance of having a baby. If I was in that situation I would be happy to have a clone made of me!

115

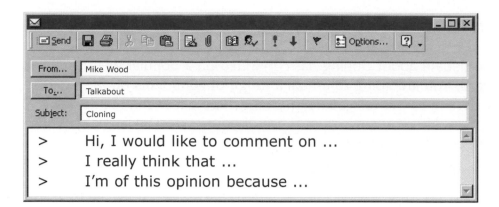

From... Mike Wood

To... Talkabout

Subject: Cloning

> Hi, I would like to comment on ...
> I really think that ...
> I'm of this opinion because ...

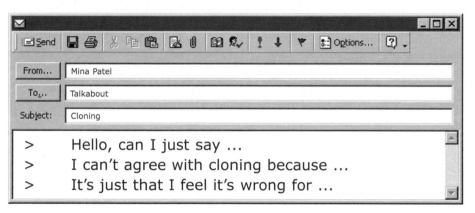

From... Mina Patel

To... Talkabout

Subject: Cloning

> Hello, can I just say ...
> I can't agree with cloning because ...
> It's just that I feel it's wrong for ...

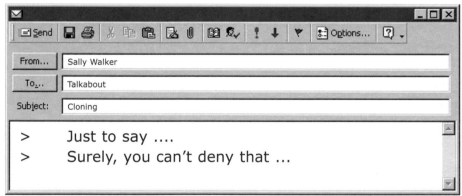

From... Sally Walker

To... Talkabout

Subject: Cloning

> Just to say ....
> Surely, you can't deny that ...

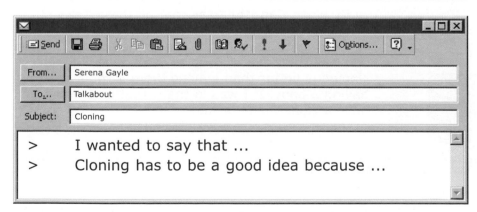

From... Serena Gayle

To... Talkabout

Subject: Cloning

> I wanted to say that ...
> Cloning has to be a good idea because ...

Review of skills

Spelling log ▶▶▶

In this section you have looked at three texts dealing with scientific topics, ranging from the newspaper article about the genetically-modified mouse to the Internet debate about human cloning. These texts contain some scientific vocabulary that you might not have encountered before.

▶ Look back at the texts that you have read in this section and pick out any words that you are unfamiliar with. Add these words to your spelling log and look up their meanings in a dictionary.

Here are some words that you might want to add to your spelling log:

Word	Definition
bizarre	
individual	
mathematician	
physique	
principle	
researcher	

You might also want to use a thesaurus to find other words that have a similar meaning.

▶ Map these out in a word-web like the one shown below:

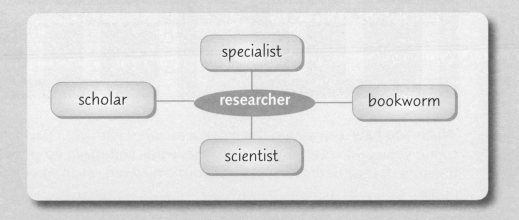

Crossword ▶▶▶

With a partner you are going to write the clues for the following crossword. Pupil A will follow the instructions in the left-hand column and pupil B the instructions in the right-hand column. Make sure that you cover up the facing column when you are working out the clues and answering the questions.

Pupil A

Find the definitions of the words across. Using the definition, work out a clue for each word. When you have got clues for all the across words in the crossword, you can see if your partner can solve the clues.

Pupil B

Find the definitions of the words down. Using the definition, work out a clue for each word. When you have got clues for all the down words in the crossword, you can see if your partner can solve the clues.

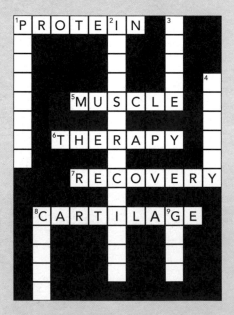

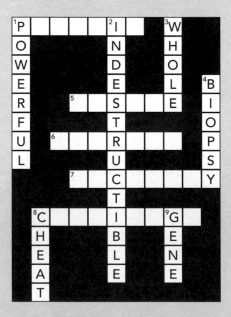

When you have completed this crossword, work with your partner to create your own crossword. Choose the words and make up clues by finding out their definitions. Try out your crossword on another pair of pupils.

Prose fiction is literature about imagined people, places and events. Writers of prose fiction have to invent an interesting setting, some believable characters and an absorbing storyline. This extract from a Sherlock Holmes story, *The Hound of the Baskervilles* by Sir Arthur Conan Doyle, has all of these. The detective Sherlock Holmes and his assistant Dr Watson are on the trail of some very strange sounds out on the moor. They are worried about the safety of Sir Henry Baskerville after a recent murder in the area.

Pre-reading

What kind of prose fiction do you enjoy reading? What do you think are the elements of a really good story?

Genre

Detective fiction, romantic novels and science-fiction stories are all examples of different types of writing. Each type of writing is called a genre and each genre has certain ingredients.

Detective fiction always has:

- a mystery that needs to be solved
- a detective who solves the mystery
- shocking or exciting passages that hold the interest of the reader.

1 Can you find each of these ingredients in the passage on the opposite page? Copy out and complete the grid below to help you record your ideas.

What is the mystery?	Who is the detective?	What turns out to be shocking?

The Hound of the Baskervilles

Again the agonised cry swept through the silent night, louder and much nearer than ever. And a new sound mingled with it, a deep, muttered rumble, musical and yet menacing, rising and falling like the low, constant murmur of the sea.

'The hound!' cried Holmes. 'Come, Watson, come! Great heavens, if we are too late!'

He had started running swiftly over the moor, and I had followed at his heels. But now from somewhere among the broken ground immediately in front of us there came one last despairing yell, and then a dull, heavy thud. We halted and listened. Not another sound broke the heavy silence of the windless night.

I saw Holmes put his hand to his forehead like a man distracted. He stamped his feet upon the ground.

'He has beaten us, Watson. We are too late.'

'No, no, surely not!'

'Fool that I was to hold my hand. And you, Watson, see what comes of abandoning your charge! But, by Heaven, if the worst has happened we'll avenge him!'

Blindly we ran through the gloom, blundering against boulders, forcing our way through gorse bushes, panting up hills and rushing down slopes, heading always in the direction whence those dreadful sounds had come. At every rise Holmes looked eagerly round him, but the shadows were thick upon the moor, and nothing moved upon its dreary face.

'Can you see anything?'

'Nothing.'

'But, hark, what is that?'

A low moan had fallen upon our ears. There it was again upon our left! On that side a ridge of rocks ended in a sheer cliff which overlooked a stone-strewn slope. On its jagged face was spread-eagled some dark, irregular object. As we ran towards it the vague outline hardened into a definite shape. It was a prostrate man face downward upon the ground, the head doubled under him at a horrible angle, the shoulders rounded and the body hunched together as if in the act of throwing a somersault. So grotesque was the attitude that I could not for the instant realise that that moan had been the passing of his soul. Not a whisper, not a rustle, rose now from the dark figure over which we stooped. Holmes laid his hand upon him and held it up again with an exclamation of horror. The gleam of the match which he struck shone upon his clotted fingers and upon the ghastly pool which widened slowly from the crushed skull of the victim. And it shone upon something else which turned our hearts sick and faint within us — the body of Sir Henry Baskerville!

From The Hound of the Baskervilles by Sir Arthur Conan Doyle

Dictionary check

agonised painful
menacing dangerous, threatening
avenge get one's own back
spread-eagled laid flat out
prostrate lying still

 Word level

Language change

The use and meanings of words change over the years. In *The Hound of the Baskervilles*, the writer uses language that sounds old-fashioned to a modern audience.

1 In the table below is a list of phrases taken from the story. Copy out and complete the table by writing down a modern version of each phrase. Use a dictionary to help you find out the meaning of any difficult words and a thesaurus to help you to choose more modern words that have the same meaning.

Old-fashioned phrase	What we would say today
1 *Great heavens, if we are too late!*	*Oh no, we'd better not be too late!*
2 *We halted and listened.*	
3 *I saw Holmes put his hand to his forehead like a man distracted.*	
4 *And you, Watson, see what comes of abandoning your charge!*	
5 *But, hark, what is that?*	
6 *A low moan had fallen on our ears*	

S Sentence Level

Fronting

Old-fashioned or **archaic** language is not only about the words and phrases that are used, but also the way that the sentences are constructed. One technique that is sometimes used is **fronting**. This is where the writer moves to the beginning of the sentence an item that doesn't belong there.

> **Example**
>
> Doyle writes
> *Again the agonised cry swept through the silent night*
> instead of
> *The agonised cry swept again through the silent night*

This has the effect of drawing the reader's attention to the word 'again' and emphasises the fact that the cry is repeated.

1 Read through the passage and pick out any examples of fronting that you can find. For each example, explain what effect the use of fronting has.

2 Write out the sentence again so that fronting does not occur. What effect does this have on the meaning of the sentence?

Freeze-framing

Watching a play or a piece of improvised drama is like looking at a sequence of moving pictures, sometimes with words and sometimes without. Actors practise their facial expressions and their bodily movements to communicate thoughts and feelings to an audience.

You are going to create three scenes from the story. These are:

- Holmes and Watson hearing in the distance the sounds of Sir Henry and then the hound
- both characters rushing to the place they think they will find Sir Henry
- their horrible discovery of the dead body.

You are going to work in a pair. One of you will play Sherlock Holmes and the other Dr Watson. Follow these steps to create three freeze-framed images:

1. Imagine you are hearing the strange sounds of Sir Henry crying out in the distance, and then a similar cry from the hound. Look at each other. Express in your face any of the following emotions:

   • surprise   • wonder   • uncertainty.

   Then freeze and hold the pose.

2. Move on, anxious to reach the source of the cries. You are eager to get to the place where you think Sir Henry is in danger. Freeze and hold the pose, using your body language to show the urgency of your movements.

3. Finally, you find the dead body of Sir Henry. Using your facial expression and body language, try to show any of the following emotions:

   • shock   • horror   • disgust.

Watch how other pupils perform their scene. How is it different from yours? Write a brief paragraph explaining what you thought were the best parts of one pair's performance. Think about the following three things:

- the body language used
- their facial expressions
- how effective their performance was.

Writing a personal response to a fiction text

When you are writing about a fiction text, you need to be able to say what you have found of interest in the text. This will require examples from the text. You are going to write an essay about the form, structure and style of the extract from *The Hound of the Baskervilles*.

Use the following writing frame to help you organise your essay:

▶ I am going to write about the form, structure and style of a passage from 'The Hound of the Baskervilles' by Sir Arthur Conan Doyle.

▶ First, Conan Doyle has chosen to use the classic ingredients of detective fiction in this extract.
The three ingredients he uses are ...

▶ These are interesting because ...

▶ Conan Doyle goes on to structure his story by dividing it into three parts. These are ...

▶ The reason I find these interesting is because ...

▶ In addition to this, the writer uses some stylistic effects to make the story interesting to read. These are ...

▶ Some examples of the words he uses are ...

▶ I find these interesting because ...

▶ To conclude, I think that the extract from 'The Hound of the Baskervilles' is effective because ...

Literature

Writing about drama involves understanding how the words can be performed on the stage, or on television and film. Plays are meant to be performed, so when reading you need to imagine the setting for the drama and how the characters might speak the words of the script.

You are going to read an extract from a comedy *The Importance of Being Earnest*, a play by Oscar Wilde. It was written in the nineteenth century when there were stricter rules over marriage in British society than there are today. Wilde was famous for creating very exaggerated comic characters, like Lady Bracknell. Here, Lady Bracknell wants to find out more about Jack Worthing before she will agree to allow him to marry her daughter.

T Text level: reading

Pre-reading

What do you think parents might want to know about somebody who wanted to marry their son or daughter? What questions do you think they would ask?

Understanding characters in context

> The humour of this extract lies in how the audience is constantly taken by surprise in the way Lady Bracknell conducts her interview of Jack Worthing. When she is told that he smokes, we expect her to disapprove. The fact that she thinks 'a man should have an occupation of some kind' is funny because it is such a bizarre idea to count smoking cigars or cigarettes as a job.

1 Lady Bracknell asks Jack a number of different questions. What are they?

2 When Jack says that he knows nothing, what is Lady Bracknell's reaction? What reason does she give for reacting in this way?

3 Why does Lady Bracknell object to Jack being found in a hand-bag at a railway station? What do you find funny about this?

4 How do you react to the characters of Lady Bracknell and Jack? What do you think their real feelings for each other are?

5 What do you think Oscar Wilde thought about the rules to do with marriage at the time he lived? Think about the following:

- the way he presents the character of Lady Bracknell
- the questions Lady Bracknell asks
- the way he makes the scene funny.

Lady Bracknell (*sitting down*) You can take a seat, Mr Worthing.

(*Looks in her pocket for note-book and pencil*)

Jack Thank you, Lady Bracknell, I prefer standing.

Lady Bracknell (*pencil and note-book in hand*) I feel bound to tell you that you are not down on my list of eligible young men, although I have the same list as the dear Duchess of Bolton has. We work together, in fact. However, I am quite ready to enter your name, should your answers be what a really affectionate mother requires. Do you smoke?

Jack Well, yes, I must admit I smoke.

Lady Bracknell I am glad to hear it. A man should always have an occupation of some kind. There are far too many idle men in London as it is. How old are you?

Jack Twenty-nine.

Lady Bracknell A very good age to be married at. I have always been of the opinion that a man who desires to get married should know either everything or nothing. Which do you know?

Jack (*after some hesitation*) I know nothing, Lady Bracknell.

Lady Bracknell I am pleased to hear it. I do not approve of anything that tampers with natural ignorance. Ignorance is like a delicate exotic fruit; touch it and the bloom is gone. The whole theory of modern education is radically unsound. Fortunately in England, at any rate, education produces no effect whatsoever. If it did, it would prove a serious danger to the upper classes, and probably lead to acts of violence in Grosvenor Square ...

Lady Bracknell Now to minor matters. Are your parents living?

Jack I have lost both my parents.

Lady Bracknell Both? ...That seems like carelessness. Who was your father? He was evidently a man of some wealth. Was he born in what the Radical papers call the purple of commerce, or did he rise from the ranks of the aristocracy?

Jack I am afraid I really don't know. The fact is, Lady Bracknell, I said I had lost my parents. It would be nearer the truth to say that my parents seem to have lost me. ... I don't actually know who I am by birth. I was ... well, I was found.

Lady Bracknell Found!

Jack The late Mr Thomas Cardew, an old gentleman of a very charitable and kindly disposition, found me, and gave me the name of Worthing, because he happened to have a first-class ticket for Worthing in his pocket at the time. Worthing is a place in Sussex. It is a seaside resort.

Lady Bracknell Where did the charitable gentleman who had a first-class ticket for this seaside resort find you?

Jack (*gravely*) In a hand-bag.

Lady Bracknell A hand-bag?

Jack (*very seriously*) Yes, Lady Bracknell. I was in a hand-bag – a somewhat large, black leather hand-bag, with handles to it – an ordinary hand-bag in fact.

Lady Bracknell In what locality did this Mr James, or Thomas, Cardew come across this ordinary hand-bag?

Jack In the cloak-room at Victoria Station. It was given to him in mistake for his own.

Lady Bracknell The cloak-room at Victoria Station?

Jack Yes. The Brighton line.

Lady Bracknell The line is immaterial. Mr Worthing, I confess I feel somewhat bewildered by what you have just told me. To be born, or at any rate bred, in a hand-bag, whether it had handles or not, seems to me to display a contempt for the ordinary decencies of family life that reminds one of the worst excesses of the French Revolution. And I presume you know what that unfortunate movement led to? As for the particular locality in which the hand-bag was found, a cloak-room at a railway station might serve to conceal a social indiscretion – has probably, indeed, been used for that purpose before now – but it could hardly be regarded as an assured basis for a recognised position in good society.

From *The Importance of Being Earnest* by Oscar Wilde

Dictionary check

radically unsound extremely mistaken
purple of commerce the class of people who earned their money in business
ranks of aristocracy the land owner classes
disposition social position
excesses outrageous behaviour

 Word level

Formal and informal language

Jack and Lady Bracknell speak to each other using the kind of **formal** language that was acceptable in the nineteenth century. However, the way people use language is constantly changing. This means that words that in the past were considered too **informal** and therefore unacceptable are nowadays seen as acceptable. This also means that other words which were once acceptable as formal language have now faded away.

1 Look up the meaning of the following words taken from the extract. Then use a thesaurus to write down the word that you would use today to give the same meaning.

a) eligible

b) idle

c) desires

d) fortunately

e) charitable

2 You can have different levels of formality in language, ranging from the very formal to the least formal. Pick out five phrases from the passage and place them on the scale below, identifying the most formal and the least formal. The first one is done for you.

most formal   You can take a seat, Mr Worthing

least formal

S Sentence level

Adopting a suitable tone

Formality does not only depend on the words that are chosen, but also the manner in which they are spoken or written. The way that we speak or write indicates our **tone** (friendly, enthusiastic, angry, etc.) and this changes depending on who we are speaking to.

1 Look at the following situations and for each one write a few sentences that adopt a suitable tone.

a) A girl explaining to a teacher why she has not done her homework.

b) A headteacher speaking in a school assembly.

c) A boy chatting to his friend about a football match.

d) A DJ on the radio talking about a hit record.

2 For each sentence you have written, say what tone you are trying to show and explain how you did this.

With a partner compare your answers and discuss how successful they are in communicating the correct tone. Think about vocabulary and sentence structures you have used.

Getting in character

When an actor plays a role in a play, he or she is not just reading the lines out but they are imagining what their character would be thinking and feeling at that time. The best actors are able to get inside the head of the person that they are playing.

You are going to work in a group of four. Two of you are going to play the parts of Jack and Lady Bracknell. These are the **actors**. The others are going to watch and, at carefully chosen moments in the scene, are going to stop the action to ask, 'What are you thinking?' These are the **stoppers**. Still speaking in character, the actors then have to explain to the stoppers what they are thinking and feeling at that moment.

You should then swap over so that the actors become stoppers and vice versa. You can even swap again so that you take different roles in the scene.

Before you begin, the actors need to consider what the characters are thinking as they speak their lines. The stoppers need to choose at least four occasions in the scene when they can stop the action.

Writing a personal response to a play

You are going to write a diary entry from the point of view of either Jack Worthing or Lady Bracknell. In the diary entry you will:

- retell the events of the scene from your character's point of view

- record your character's personal feelings about meeting the other for the first time.

Before you start writing the diary entry, remind yourself about the thoughts and feelings that the actor(s) playing your character had in the speaking and listening activity. Make notes about what your character would have thought and felt at key moments in the scene. Use the planning frame below to develop your ideas.

At the start of the scene

Would your character be nervous or impatient? Would he or she be happy to see the other or have a poor opinion of them?

When they are talking

Does your character get on well with the other character at the start? What does your character think about what the other says? Does the conversation change at all?

At the end of the scene

How does your character feel? Angry, upset, amused or sad?

After you have finished planning you are now ready to write your diary entry. Use one of the writing frames on page 134 to help you.

Lady Bracknell's diary

Today I met Jack Worthing for the first time. He is the man who ...

Before I met him I felt ...

I started my interview of him by asking ...

When he replied that he did, I thought ...

I think that ...

I then went on to ask him ... and his reply was ...

I was also impressed when he told me that ...

I don't believe that education ...

However, his next reply was quite shocking because ...

Overall, I believe this man ...

Jack Worthing's diary

Today I met Lady Bracknell for the first time. She is ...

Before I met her I felt ...

She started by asking me ...

I thought this was ... and replied ...

I think that ...

She then went on to ask me ... and I replied ...

I think she was impressed when I told her that ...

At this point I thought that the interview was going quite well and I felt ...

However, things started to go wrong when Lady Bracknell asked me ...

When I told her the truth her reaction was ... This made me feel ...

Overall, my feelings about Lady Bracknell are ...

Help box

Remember to use formal language and try to adopt an appropriate tone for the situation.

Literature

Poetry is a form of literature that expresses feeling, images and ideas through the careful choice of language. A poem is a very personal piece of communication and writing about poetry is a skill that takes practice. Sometimes the meaning of a poem isn't immediately clear, but if you look closely at it you should be able to make sense of it. Looking at the words the poet uses and deciding what they say to you can help you to understand the poem. The poems you are going to read are both about cats, but as you will see, they are very different types of poem.

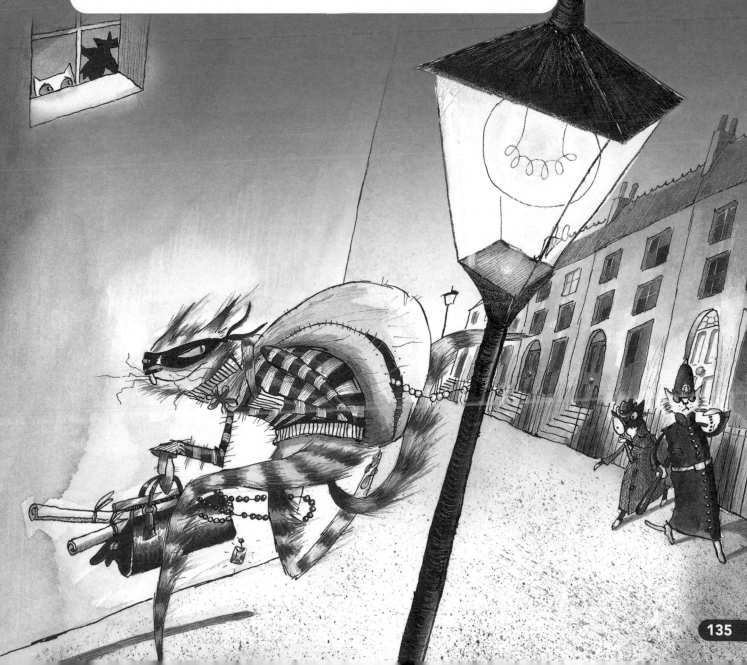

135

Pre-reading

Would you write a poem about a cat? Which features or characteristics of a cat would you draw the reader's attention to?

Investigating word choices

1 Briefly explain what you learn about both types of cat in these two poems.

2 Write down a list of words that show the personality of both cats. Compare your list with a partner. Did you choose any of the same words?

3 Which of the two cats do you prefer? Give reasons for your answer.

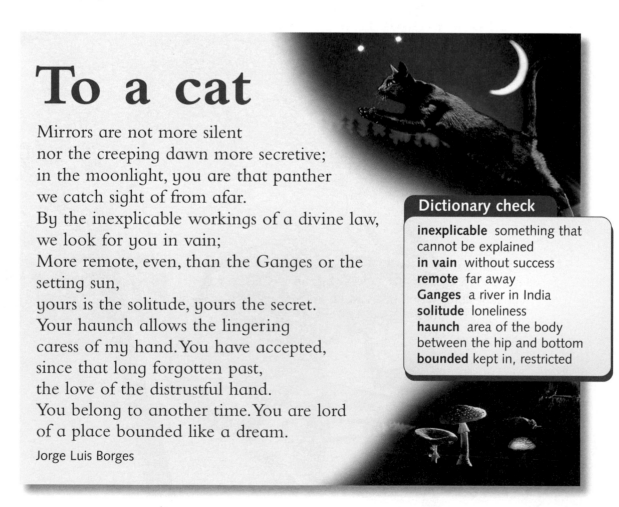

To a cat

Mirrors are not more silent
nor the creeping dawn more secretive;
in the moonlight, you are that panther
we catch sight of from afar.
By the inexplicable workings of a divine law,
we look for you in vain;
More remote, even, than the Ganges or the setting sun,
yours is the solitude, yours the secret.
Your haunch allows the lingering
caress of my hand. You have accepted,
since that long forgotten past,
the love of the distrustful hand.
You belong to another time. You are lord
of a place bounded like a dream.

Jorge Luis Borges

Dictionary check

inexplicable something that cannot be explained
in vain without success
remote far away
Ganges a river in India
solitude loneliness
haunch area of the body between the hip and bottom
bounded kept in, restricted

Macavity: the mystery cat

Macavity's a Mystery Cat: he's called the Hidden Paw –
For he's the master criminal who can defy the Law.
He's the bafflement of Scotland Yard, the Flying Squad's despair:
For when they reach the scene of crime – Macavity's not there!

Macavity, Macavity, there's no one like Macavity,
He's broken every human law, he breaks the law of gravity.
His powers of levitation would make a fakir stare,
And when you reach the scene of crime – Macavity's not there!
You may seek him in the basement, you may look up in the air –
But I tell you once and once again, Macavity's not there!

Macavity's a ginger cat, he's very tall and thin;
You would know him if you saw him, for his eyes are sunken in.
His brow is deeply lined with thought, his head is highly domed;
His coat is dusty from neglect, his whiskers are uncombed.
He sways his head from side to side, with movements like a snake;
And when you think he's half asleep, he's always wide awake.

Macavity, Macavity, there's no one like Macavity,
For he's a fiend in feline shape, a monster of depravity.
You may meet him in a by-street, you may see him in the square –
But when a crime's discovered, then Macavity's not there!

He's outwardly respectable. (They say he cheats at cards.)
And his footprints are not found in any file of Scotland Yard's.
And when the larder's looted, or the jewel-case is rifled,
Or when the milk is missing, or another Peke's been stifled,
Or the greenhouse glass is broken, and the trellis past repair –
Ay, there's the wonder of the thing! Macavity's not there!

And when the Foreign Office find a Treaty's gone astray,
Or the Admiralty lose some plans and drawings by the way,
There may be a scrap of paper in the hall or on the stair –
But it's useless to investigate – Macavity's not there!
And when the loss has been disclosed, the Secret Service say:
'It must have been Macavity!' – but he's a mile away.
You'll be sure to find him resting, or a-licking of his thumbs,
Or engaged in doing complicated long division sums.

Macavity, Macavity, there's no one like Macavity,
There never was a Cat of such deceitfulness and suavity.
He always has an alibi, and one or two to spare:
At whatever time the deed took place – MACAVITY WASN'T THERE!
And they say that all the Cats whose wicked deeds are widely known
(I might mention Mungojerrie, I might mention Griddlebone)
Are nothing more than agents for the Cat who all the time
Just controls their operations: the Napoleon of Crime!

T.S.Eliot

Dictionary check

defy stand up to
bafflement frustration
levitation magical ability to float in the air
fakir holy man
feline cat qualities
depravity wickedness
suavity confident

Poetic vocabulary

You are going to look at the use of rhythm and rhyme in 'Macavity: the Mystery Cat'. Eliot uses a very regular rhythm in this poem. Having a regular rhythm means that the number of syllables in each of the lines is roughly the same. This helps the poem to flow smoothly as we read it.

Example

In the first line the syllables are as follows: (15)

Ma-cav-i-ty's-a-Mys-ter-y-Cat-he's-called-the-Hid-den Paw

1 Check the first and second verses by counting up the syllables.

2 What do you notice about the number of syllables in each of the lines?

3 What effect do you think Eliot achieves by using this regular rhythm in the poem?

Eliot also uses a lot of rhyming words at the end of lines in this poem. This means that the words at the end of the lines sound the same or similar. For example, the end word of the first line 'Paw' rhymes with the end word of the second line 'Law'. When two lines in a poem rhyme like this we call them a **rhyming couplet**.

4 Write down the rhymes used at the end of the lines in the second verse. How many rhyming couplets can you find in the third verse of the poem?

5 What does Eliot achieve by using rhyme in this poem? Pick out one example of the poet's use of rhyme and explain why you like it.

Now you are going to look at the use of metaphor and personification in 'To a Cat'. Giving human qualities to a thing or object is an example of a poetic technique called **personification**.

> Example
>
> *Mirrors are not more silent*

6 Borges describes the 'mirrors' as 'silent' and the 'dawn' as 'creeping'. What do you think he is saying about the cat when it appears in the morning after being out all night?

7 Match the things with the actions to create examples of personification that match the meanings in the third column.

Thing	Doing action(s)	Meaning of personification
a) The sun	cut through me	The car engine started.
b) The door	leapt off the page	The word came to my attention easily.
c) The word	coughed and spluttered into life	The wind was extremely cold.
d) The wind	smiled on us	The door was wide open.
e) The car engine	yawned open	The sun shone brightly for us.

Poets sometimes describe something that is unfamiliar to the reader by comparing it to something that the reader knows about. A word that is used to compare things like this is called a **metaphor**.

> Example
>
> When Borges writes '   *you are that panther*' he is comparing the cat to a panther.

8 Why do you think Borges compares the cat to a panther? Think about the qualities that a panther has. Borges also compares the cat to a lord. Why?

Formal and informal language

The two poems on pages 136 and 137 contrast quite sharply in their use of formal and informal language. One way in which we can see this is the informal use of language that Eliot employs in 'Macavity: the Mystery Cat' and the more formal style chosen by Borges in 'To a Cat'.

1 Contracting words from their full form is often a sign that a writer is using an informal style. For example, in the first verse of Eliot's poem, the words 'he is' are contracted to read 'he's'. This makes the poem more relaxed in the way it is read and suggests a lighthearted tone. Are there any other examples of this informal style?

2 The poem by Borges has a much more formal style because of the very proper way the poet seems to be addressing the cat. The following lines are examples of the formal style used in the poem. Next to each example, rewrite the line by contracting the words and using an apostrophe.

Line from the poem (formal)	Rewritten from the poem (informal)
You are that panther	
You have accepted	
You are the lord	

3 With a partner, discuss why you think each poet chose to use either a formal or an informal style. Write down your reasons.

SL Speaking and listening

Performing a poem

Work in a group of four. You are going to perform one of the poems you have read to the other members of your class. Here are some ways you could try performing the poem:

• Read a line or two lines each at a time.

• Two of you share the reading of the poem, while the other two act the 'characters' in the poem.

• Record your reading of the poem on tape or set the poem to music.

• Read the poem as a rap and accompany your reading with dance movements.

Try to capture the mood of the poem through the tone of voice you use and the way you speak the lines.

Writing a response to a poem

You are going to write about one of the poems you have read in this unit. Choose one and ask yourself what interests you about the poem. The notes that you have made will be helpful. Use the planning frame to help you to organise your ideas:

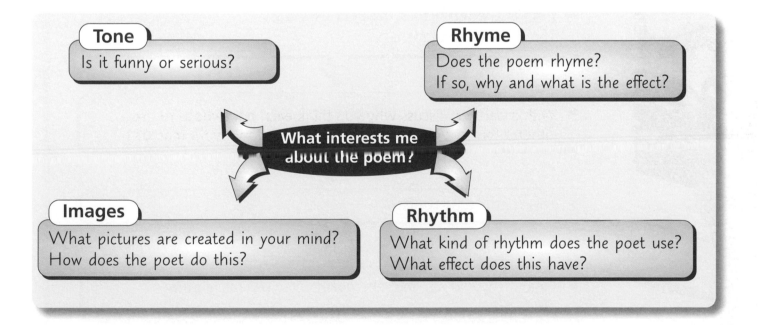

Tone
Is it funny or serious?

Rhyme
Does the poem rhyme?
If so, why and what is the effect?

What interests me about the poem?

Images
What pictures are created in your mind?
How does the poet do this?

Rhythm
What kind of rhythm does the poet use?
What effect does this have?

You are now going to write your personal response to the poem as a critical essay. Use the writing frame to help you to structure your writing.

▶ I have chosen to write about the poem ... by ...

▶ There are ... reasons why I have chosen to write about this poem.
▶ Firstly, the poem has a ... tone. This is because ...

▶ Secondly, the poet uses interesting images in the poem.
For example ...

▶ This picture is interesting because ...

▶ Another image he uses is ...
▶ I like this because ...

▶ One of the techniques the poet uses is ...
The poet says the cat is ...

▶ This captures my attention because I can just imagine ...
Another technique he uses is ...

▶ This is striking because ...

▶ Finally, I would say that the poem ... for several reasons.
These are ...

Reading log ▶▶▶

In this section you have read extracts from a piece of prose fiction by Sir Arthur Conan Doyle; a play by Oscar Wilde and poems by T. S. Eliot and Jorge Luis Borges. Add these titles to your reading log.

▶ You could then look for other stories, plays or poems by the authors or poets that you have read in this section.

If you have enjoyed reading a particular genre of literature in this section, such as detective fiction or comedy, you might want to look for other titles in this genre. Ask your teacher to recommend other books that you might enjoy. Libraries sometimes keep books of a certain genre together, so you could find all the detective books in a special section. The librarian will be able to help you to find the type of book you are looking for.

▶ As you add to your reading log, you could build up a reading-web for the genre of writing you enjoy. Use this technique to map out the different titles that you have read.

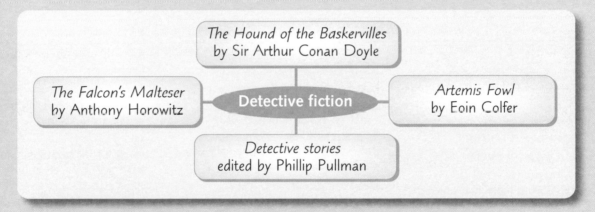

Making connections ▶▶▶

You are going to play this game in a group of four. One member of the team will play the quiz-master and ask the questions. Two people will play together as the blue team and one person will play alone as the white team. The contestants must make sure that they cover up the questions at the bottom of the page.

The quiz-master will ask the questions and the teams can buzz in to answer. Getting the question right turns the question space to your team's colour. The aim of the game is to fill in the spaces so that a continuous line of your team's colour goes across the board, either horizontally for the blue team or vertically for the white team. The team that gets the question right gets to choose the next letter or combination of letters.

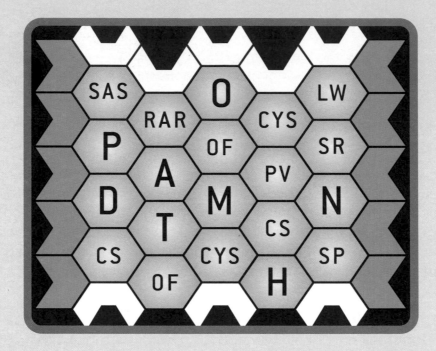

Questions ▶▶▶

P
What 'P' is used to organise a piece of writing?

What 'P' is placed at the start of a word to make new word?

D
What 'D' is a clause that relies on another clause in order to make sense?

What 'D' is a type of journal?

H
What 'H' is a word that sounds the same as another word?

What 'H' is a linking word that has the same meaning as 'but'?

A
What 'A' describes a noun?

Which 'A' is a voice where the subject performs the action of the verb?

T
What 'T' are past, present and future all types of?

What 'T' is a sentence that sums up what a paragraph is about?

O
Which 'O' usually comes after the subject and the verb in a sentence?

Which 'O' is given to a word that sounds the same as its meaning?

M
What 'M' is the name given to the clause in a sentence that could stand alone?

What 'M' is another name given to the kind of atmosphere a writer creates?

N
What 'N' can be a person, place or thing?

What 'N' do you make when planning a piece of writing?

SR
What 'SR' means to look over quickly?

SP
What 'SP' is placed around the words people say when they are written down?

LW
Which 'LW' are used to join ideas in one sentence to another?

PV
What 'PV' means that the subject moves to the end of the sentence and becomes the agent?

CYS
What 'CYS' do you do when you want to find out if you've got reliable information?

SAC
Which 'SAC' are usually introduced at the beginning of a story?

FT
What 'FT' is used to describe verbs that have 'will' or 'shall' in front of them?

CS
What 'CS' is made up of different clauses?

OF
What 'OF' could be used to describe archaic language?

RAR
Which 'RAR' do poets look at when they are thinking about how their poems will sound?